FARMING TECHNOLOGY BRINGS

SOCIAL ADVANAGES

JOHN LOK

Copyright © John Lok
All Rights Reserved.

This book has been published with all efforts taken to make the material error-free after the consent of the author. However, the author and the publisher do not assume and hereby disclaim any liability to any party for any loss, damage, or disruption caused by errors or omissions, whether such errors or omissions result from negligence, accident, or any other cause.

While every effort has been made to avoid any mistake or omission, this publication is being sold on the condition and understanding that neither the author nor the publishers or printers would be liable in any manner to any person by reason of any mistake or omission in this publication or for any action taken or omitted to be taken or advice rendered or accepted on the basis of this work. For any defect in printing or binding the publishers will be liable only to replace the defective copy by another copy of this work then available.

Copyright

Contents

Preface

Introduction

Farming industry is important food industry, farming industry may include farming products and non-farming products, it may include: farming of wheat, fruit, meat,corn , cotton etc.food and non-food products. So, any countries governments and farmers ought need to concern how to learn farming technology to improve and help them to achieve farming economic development. In my this book, I shall attempt to explain what farming technology means and how learning farming technology can help any countries to bring economy growth , how raising farming and non-farming productivities to bring farmer individual profit methods.

I shall concentrate on research China and India and developing coutnries and developed countries, UK, US farming industry ought how to improve their faming technology in order to raise farming productivities. This book is suitable to any students like to learn what farming economy concept is and how farming technology ought to be improved to achieve farming products and non-farming products productivities.

In my this book, I shall attempt to indicate future farming development customer needs problems . I also apply demand and supply theory to explain the developed countries' low wage growth how to influence food quality demand .

Prologue

growth
● Which farming aspects will influence GDP growth
● How does the tea agriculture sector affect the Malawi economy? p.61-79
Chapter 4
Economists opinions to old and new economic social development
● the invisible hand theory
● the division of labour concept
● Surplus value of labour theory
How applying economy theories solve economic problems
The problem of full employment of resources (the division of labour concept and Surplus value of labour theory)

Five bases problems of economy
rational consumer theory p.80-110
Demand And Supply elastic Theory Solves Consumer Problems

Supply and demand and price elasticities principle predict oil energy user behaviour
Demand and supply principle can misuse to predict consumer behaviour when the two firms participate advertisement to promote their products in the same time

Demand and supply principle predict public transport tool passenger behaviour
Supply and demand principle explains Why has it relationship between immigration to US these two regions immigrant number and wage?

Rationing by prices theory p.111-125

New Economic Consumer Choice Theory
Solves Consumer Problems

What is 'consumer choice theory'?
How to spply consumer choice theory to
predict Consumer Behavior Marketing at
Apple Computer p.126-140
Microeconomics Models and Theories
solve customer problems
Developed countries low skillful labour
market wage grows up causing
factors
labour market excess supply and shortage demand
factor
● the division of labour concept
● Surplus value of labour theory

Refugee immigration factor
Technological development factor

Second part
behavioral economy predicts
consumer behavior

CHAPTER I

Introduction to farming industry development

Learning agricultural economic advantages

What is agricultural economic? What is farming? Why do we need to learn agricultural economy? Farming is an organized way to produce food., bio-energy and other non-food foods by cultivation. Agricultural economies deals with how to organize other non-foods; how the products are distributed, handled and consumed; and with the local and global impact this has on living conditions, societies, environment and economies. Also, farming and argicultural economic has close relationship.When global farming development can be kept the best, then it will bring every farmer has good income, even the country's economy will be also improved.

Farming can be defined as an organized way to grow crops and rear animals in order to provide food, bio-energy and other non-foods through cultivation with the purpose of selling the products, or using them in kind. Our definition of farming includes all kinds of animal farming and plant farming everywhere, irrespective
of location aims of production, methods of production, economy and society. It refers to all kinds of outdoor crop cultivation, plus greenhouse cultivation, and forms of animal food. We won't exclude fish farming. Farming activities include all kinds of form work that is conducted

with or without the help of machinery and equipment, such as tractor driving control of automatic milking, field inspections, equipment repairs, digging ditches, mending fences, carrying feed and water for farm

animals, making budgets and discussion with agricultural advises. Finally, agriculture aovers a wider field than farming , for example in formulations , such as

agricultural production, agricultural sectors and politics.

Agriculture is whether a meeting between nature and human society? Whehter is necessary for human survival? Is it dependent on land, is ruled by weather, seasons and biological rhythms, is both predictable and unpredictable, economizing with resources, is conducted by large numbers of farmers, and may be highly influenced by social and cultural factors? Why is agriculture both predictable and unpredictable? Because seasonality influences practical farming, agricultural business and food consumption. If the harvest fails, one generally has to wait for the right season before it is possible to start all cover again, for example, on grazing seasons. Seasonality thus characrerizes much of farm work and yearly rhythm in farming. So, the season may impacts supply and demand for agricultural products, and price levels on inputs as sowing seed, and outputs , such as grains and meats.Hence, farming's dependency on nature means that agriculture is both highly predictable and unpredictable. Days and seasons come and go, which gives farming a repetitive and foreseeable character. Both crop farming and livestock production are in ordinary weather patterns and seasons. Prolonged rainy seasons can delay seedinf and distrurb the entire growing season.

Why do farmers need to choose how to use degree of farming market orientation? Some kinds of farming are certainly much more frequent in some parts of the world trhan in others,for example, find both big commercial farms and poor smallholdings in Kenya, India, China and Braxil. There may also be homogenous farmung on plains where farmers have more in common with colleagues across border than with smallholders in other parts of the same country. So, China, INdia, Brazil and Kenya farmers need to choose where grow good taste food, fruit , vegetable in order to make wrong farming land investment loss.

What is food chain relationship? A food chain can be defined as a linear sequential structure that shows varios stages along the processes of production, handling and consumption of food. The food chain approach is widely applied, and a way to involve , such as the farmer, the transport sector and the consumer. It is also appliable to fibre, bio-energy and other non-food chains that are being produced in a agricultural sector. However, the chains for marketed foods is complex. On input supply hand, the purchased input resources that are put into the food chain. Among the input suppliers to farm production, such as fertilizer industries, seed companies, animal feed companies, farm machinery companies, agro-chemical industries,petrochemical companies and electricity suppliers. Energy and chemicals are also continuously required during later stages, which also use large amounts of inputs, such as packaging materials, transport and storage facilities. Then farmers are main the market oriented farm production of crops role and animal products, fibres, bio-energy and varying by-products form the basis for food chains and other agricultural chains role both.

The intermediate stages include larger or smaller parts of the total handling and final costs for agricultural product. SOme of these activities are frequently repeated along the chain, not least transport, repackaging and intermediate storeage. It includes these processes, such as post-harvest processes, storage , transport, distribution, wholesale, food processing, such as change and/or preserve foods, packaging and retailing. The final stage is consumption , or eating, it relates to consumer individual food purchase choice activities, such as the trip to the supermarket, storing in the household and cooking, and eventually alos some care with packaging and food waste.

However, waste is produced all along the chain, and is a by-products to foods. The distination between waste and by-products may be a some that to a great extent is decided by the ambition to reuse or recycle. Nonetheless, waste occurs, stored in landfills and/or emitted into air and water. Consequently, waste can cause air and water pollution to our natural environment. For example, HOng Kong city is not a good place to develop farming industry. The reasons may include: air and water is polluted seriously, the numebr of people living in urban areas had exceed the number of people in countryside in Hong Kong city, due to population had been increasing from Chinese emmigrants every day. Hence, HOng KOng';s agriculture development is worse and difficult to compare prior 1960. Moreover, HOng JOng has many people need to live, so many lands had been using to build houses, because HOng KOng is a small city, land shortage is serious. So, shortage of land supply and ships' gas emission and cars' fuels pollutes Hong KOng seas, rivers, and air. Hence, these HOng Kong
people's activities, manufacturers' pollution activites on manufacturing processes, shipping transport's oil emission activities , even air planes flying activities had influenced Hong KOng can not provide good natural environment to carry on farming activities in order to grow up its

agricultural economic development again easily after 1960. Also, it means that Hong KOng's land used for permanent crops won't have possible to develop again. It is HOng KOng government's duty. It only considers housing, financial activities aspect, but it neglects to research how to continue to develop its farming activities in order to bring agricultural economic growth, such as before 1960's successful agricultural development on rural.

Why do we need to know where can provide enough livestosk food to eat and good climate environment farming land use? The reason is simple, global population is continue increasing, such as China, India. They are increasing many people , they feel needs to live in themselves countries, if they can not know how to find the best farming lands to grow food, vegetables , fruits
or let livestock to alive. Then, the future food shortage challenges may occur to cause these countries have many people die because global has no enough foods to supply to them to eat in possible. So, studies of farm animals around the world teach is to the most varied types of landscapes and places, such as windblown moorlands, muddy backyards and enornous pigs or chickens, plants. SOme of kinds of animal farming are based on vast land areas, such as nomadism and large-scale rearing of sheep or cattle on low yielding pastures.

IN constrast, scientists find increasing numbers of plants with tens of thousands of pigs or chickens, to which the feed is transported from far away. So, seeking the best farming lands will be needed to any countries farmers in order to raise farming foods productive number more easily. The lands have enough water, none dry weater. Then, the land will be a good farming or harrested more easily. Farmers also need to know how to solve environmental problems to influence various kinds of livestock production.

They may include (1) how to directly connected with animals, such as emissions of greenhouse gases, such as carbon dioxide and methane from ruminants; emissions of nitrous oxide from animal manure; overgrazing, causing soil erosion and reduced biodiversity; leakage of nutrients from animal manure into water courses, high consumption of water, especially by high producing dairy cattles. (2) connected with feed production, it may include: Emissions of greenhouse, gases due to methods of cultivation; ;and degraduation due to eventual exploitation of forests and permanent pastures; problems due to use; overuse; of fertilizer and pesticides; water problems due to irrigation of feed crops, (3) connected with other parts of the food chain, it may include: Emissions from transportation, cooling, processing and packaging along the animal food chain.

Current trends in global livestock production need must increase. The reasons may include that the world has experienced large-scale increases in demand food of animal origin , when increased world population, increased per capita consumption of animal foods, increased livestock production need, partly on the basis of highly resource intensive methods of production, increased attention to the livestock sector's negative impact on climate change, increased attention to the livestock sector's negative impact on other environmental problems, increased attention to the value of animal
production for reducing poverty and generating cash income and developing smallholder farming needs.

Another learning agricultural economic reason, instead of solution to above farming land shortage and environment pollution influences difficult growing foods reason. The reason is learning how to increase agricultural production of non-foods. Agricultural non-food production includes all kinds of products that are obtained through farming for other purposes than to be eaten. Dealing with agricultural non-food production includes a plathre of different activites, such as : production of commodities, utilization of by-products, recycling of organic matter, various agricultural related service and extraaction of bio-energy.

Bearing in mind, that one-third of the global land area is agricultural land(plus another one-third of forest land), farming is involved in flows of energy and i ncontinuous growth of enormous quantities of organic substances in the form of vegetable and animal matter. This gives thew agricultural sector a unique position in the border land between agriculture, energy and other natural resources. IN this perspective, human may perceive the farmed landscape as an area for the production with more or less ambitious utilization of by-products and recycling of resources plus numerous other beneficial activities. For example, natural fibes from crop and other plants contribute to substantial parts of the entire agricultural non-food production. For another example, in cotton farming, connon lint is ususally the main purpose, with cotton seed as by-product , although both are highly valuable. Other plant fibes are of more typical by-product character. COir fibes from coconuts, for another example, are quite useful for mats and brushes, but hardly the primary motive for coconut production. IN addition, fibre crops generate straw and husks at early stages of the fibre chains and further along the chains other fibrous residues may be achieved. SOme of these may be used in animal husbandry, as building material or compested to be cycled back into the land. At the same time as some of the traditional use of fibres is replaced by plastics, new fields of application are being developed , such as mixtures between natural and synthetic fibes for industrial purposes.

However, cotton is globally traded and an important commodity in the world economy with regard to both the fibres and its valuable oil and protein rich cotton seed. IN addition, cotton is also important at regional and local levels, like many other plant fibres. According to FAOSTAT, the largeest amount of cotton lint was in 2009 produced by China, with India , in second place, US in third and Pakistan as number four. Taken together, the four leading cotton producing countries allounteed for much as 72 per cent of the total quantity.

On conclusion, following above issues , they explain that learning agricultural econmy can also help any countries' non-food farming production farming industry, instead of food farming production development. Hence, it will be our future any countries and farmers duties to learn how to develop agriculture in order to make the best choice to achieve the maximum non-farming food or farming food production to bring global human living benefits.

● Farming economy researchs

Agricultural economics, study of the allocation, distribution, and utilization of the resources used, along with the commodities produced, by farming. Agricultural economics plays a role in the economics of development, for a continuous level of farm surplus is one of the wellsprings of technological and commercial growth.

Farmers have always had to worry about economics. At what price can they sell their produce? Will buying new dairy cows pay off in having more milk to sell? What's the going rate for farm labor? However, agricultural economics, meaning establishing general principles and scientific rules to answer such questions, didn't develop until the late 19th or early 20th century.While some economists focus on theory, the importance of agricultural economics is that it's an applied discipline, not just academic. Farmers need information that helps them stay afloat financially, and the various types of agricultural economics tackle the relevant issues. In general, one can say that when a large fraction of a country's population depends on agriculture for its livelihood, average incomes are low. That does not mean that a country is poor because most of its population is engaged in agriculture; it is closer to the truth to say that because a country is poor, most of its people must rely upon agriculture for a living.

In general, farmers and economists will like to resesrch these questions or concern these questions when farmers grow their farming business or farming economist research how farming industry brings our global economic influences, these questions may include: What are the production costs of agriculture? How can farmers manage them successfully? How can farmers use their land and their workforce most effectively? Do the costs of buying equipment outweigh the profits of greater mechanized efficiency? As demands change, such as the growing interest in organic produce, is it necessary or profitable for farmers to change what they grow or how they produce it? How can society balance the needs of farmers with those of hikers, dirt bikers and other outdoor-recreation enthusiasts? How do we balance the needs of farmers with the needs of the environment? What should government farm policy entail? etc. different questions. For example, if a family's income were to increase by 100 percent, the amount it would spend on food might increase by 60 percent; if formerly its expenditures on food had been 50 percent of its budget, after the increase they would amount to only 40 percent of its budget. It follows that as incomes increase, a smaller fraction of the total resources of society is required to produce the amount of food demanded by the population.

How farming industry develops ? That fact would have surprised most economists of the early 19th century, who feared that the limited supply of land in the populated areas of Europe would determine the continent's ability to feed its growing population. Their fear was based on the so-called law of diminishing returns: that under given conditions an increase in the amount of labour and capital applied to a fixed amount of land results in a less-than-proportional increase in the output of food. That principle is a valid one, but what the classical economists could not foresee was the extent to which the state of the arts and the methods of production would change. Some of the changes occurred in agriculture; others occurred in other sectors of the economy but had a major effect on the supply of food.

In looking back upon the history of the more developed countries, one can see that agriculture has played an important part in the process of their enrichment. For one thing, if development is to occur, agriculture must be able to produce a surplus of food to maintain the growing nonagricultural labour force. Since food is more essential for life than are the services provided by merchants or bankers or factories, an economy cannot shift to such activities unless food is available for barter or sale in sufficient quantities to support those engaged in them. Unless food can be obtained through international trade, a country does not normally develop industrially until its farm areas can supply its towns with food in exchange for the products of their factories.

Economic development also requires a growing labour force. In an agricultural country most of the workers needed must come from the rural population. Thus agriculture must not only supply a surplus of food for the towns, but it must also be able to produce the increased amount of food with a relatively smaller labour force. It may do so by substituting animal power for human power or by gradually introducing labour-saving machinery.

Agriculture may also be a source of the capital needed for industrial development to the extent that it provides a surplus that may be converted into the funds needed to purchase industrial equipment or to build roads and provide public services. For those reasons, a country seeking to develop its economy may be well advised to give a significant priority to agriculture. Experience in the developing countries has shown that agriculture can be made much more productive with the proper investment in irrigation systems, research, fertilizers, insecticides, and herbicides.

Like many economic disciplines, the agricultural economics definition stretches to a wide variety of fields and career paths. Agribusiness addresses issues in marketing, farm management, agricultural finance and trade. Policy analysts look at the effect of government agricultural policy on farms. Market researchers study market conditions to gauge the sales potential of different farm products. So, farming economic may include these aspects of research

1 Rural development and regional economics

2 Supply chain study and management

3 Natural resource economics, which studies how farmers

can get the maximum use out of their land and other resources

4 Risk analysis

● Factors may bring risks to any farmers.

1 Time and Change external environment factor

Farming has always had an element of risk: One bad harvest or a crop blight can ruin a farm. However, the economics have changed over the centuries. At one time, increasing farm production was done entirely by expanding the amount of agricultural land: double the size of the farm, double the yields. Now, however, land is harder to come by, so farmers rely more on high-yield crops, machinery and the use of fertilizer. Another change is that governments in the 20th century became much more involved in controlling prices for produce. Agricultural prices fluctuate due to yield, supply and demand, so stabilizing prices and ensuring that farmers stay in business became a government priority.

2 Economic Factors Affecting Farming

Although farming is one of the world's oldest professions, modern farming is affected by uniquely modern economic factors. Farmers today compete in a complex economic environment where customers choose from produce grown all over the world and governments provide financial incentives for the production of certain crops rather than others. Although independently minded growers manage to create markets of their own through direct sales and other creative strategies, the majority of American farmers are still at the mercy of both economic factors and the weather.

Commodity Prices

The price of major commodity crops such as corn and soy depends of a variety of factors, such as investor speculation, weather and demand for these crops for both food and nonfood uses such as biofuels. Farmers who grow commodity crops earn or lose money based on the current rate that industrial buyers will pay for their output. In addition, commodity prices are affected by international economic factors, such as the weakness or strength of the dollar, because these farmers are competing with American farmers as well as with growers from all over the world.

Subsidies

The American government pays subsidies to farmers who grow commodity crops such as corn and soy because modern federal agricultural policy is based on the assumption that agricultural mass production benefits the economy by keeping food prices low. In theory, this policy provides farmers with a measure of economic stability, and provides consumers with affordable prices on the many processed food products made from these commodity crops. This policy encourages farmers to create an oversupply of a narrow range of crops because they make money for growing these foods regardless of current market conditions.

Labor and Immigration Laws

For better or for worse, mainstream agriculture depends on poorly paid labor that is often performed by migrant farmers, who are frequently living in the country illegally. The work pays so little that most naturally born citizens are unwilling to do it. If we are to continue buying agricultural produce at the prices to which we have grown accustomed, we must rely on workers who will work for the low wages that are customary in the field. Farming is affected by immigration laws that influence the availability of labor, as well as labor laws that allow or disallow subsistence agricultural wages.

What risks and opportunities corn or cotton farmers need

to concern ? The cotton industry is huge, with cotton grown in dozens of countries around the world. Becoming a cotton farmer on a small scale is easier than starting a commercially viable farm that can compete with the enormous operations that already control the market. Cotton is a crop that requires lots of hot weather, so it is only viable in southern locations. Buy land that is suitable for growing cotton. corn farmer will need a location with a lot of hot, sunny weather and access to water. If a corn farmer is growing cotton as a hobby or for personal use, his farm doesn't need to be very large. If the corn farmer is attempting to make a living as a cotton farmer, he will need to profit from economies of scale, and will require at least 100 acres of land. This can be done on the job by working on a cotton farm and how operate the cotton plant, or more formally by attending an agricultural college and pursuing an advanced degree in agriculture. Learning by trial and error can be an expensive proposition in agriculture; the more the corn farmer learns in advance from the experience of others, the more likely the corn farmer is to avoid expensive mistakes. Plant the cotton farmer cotton seeds and provide them with all the requirements for them to thrive, including fertile soil, water and sunshine. Conventional cotton growing involves the use of large amounts of pesticides and herbicides. Decide if this the route what the cotton farmer wants to pursue, or if he wants to attempt to grow organic cotton. Growing organically is more labor-intensive, but the cotton farmer can sell his crop at a higher price. Develop a working relationship with suppliers and buyers. Agriculture is a competitive business, and any cotton farmers will need connections and a good reputation to sell their crop every year for a good price.

What are fish farming risks and opportunities ? Fish farming is a hot topic in some circles. Environmentalists are often critical of the impact fish farms can have on the environment, while advocates point out that they're a crucial source of high-quality protein. Wherever fish farmers stand on that debate, one of the big advantages of fish farming is that it's a fine entrepreneurial opportunity.

The Fundamental Problem which any fish farmers will be possible to encounter, they may include: Fish farming exists to address a fundamental problem, the demand for fish as a food source grows as the human population grows, and the number of fish available in the wild isn't keeping pace. Even in carefully managed wild fisheries, the combination of climate change, pollution and pressure from fishermen can produce unpredictable variations in the supply of fish. In a worst-case scenario, that can cause a fish population to crash, as Atlantic cod did in the 1970s and 1980s. In the long term, expecting conventional fisheries to continue to meet the world's needs with wild fish is as unrealistic as expecting a network of hunters to keep supermarket meat cases filled. Fish farming, or aquaculture as it's formally known, will need to make up the difference.

Fish farming risk

1 Keeps Fish Affordable

One of the basic principles of economics is that if demand is increasing and the supply is not, costs will go up. Over time, that trend could make fish unaffordable for all but the affluent. Bucking that trend is one of the biggest advantages of fish farming. By providing a steady, reliable, high-volume supply of fish, it helps the price remain manageable for most shoppers.

2 Reliable Supply and Wide Distribution

Having a reliable supply of fish is another advantage of

aquaculture. The wild fishery fluctuates naturally, with catches rising or falling by the day, month or season. Fish farms turn out predictable harvests of fish at consistent sizes, making it easy for chefs, supermarkets, fishmongers and individual customers to plan their purchases. For restaurants and processors, this consistency means they can easily provide portions in standard sizes, too. Another advantage of fish farming is that it brings the supply of fish to where the consumers are. From open pens in inland lakes to tanks and ponds on dry land, fish farms can be set up almost anywhere there's a market. This cuts the financial and environmental cost of shipping and provides consumers with fresher fish. That's a win-win.

3 Consumer Health

Health authorities worldwide encourage more fish consumption, including the USDA's Dietary Guidelines for Americans, because it's a high-quality protein source that's low in saturated fat. Salmon has the added advantage of being especially high in omega-3 fatty acids, which promote heart health. Switching just a few meals per week from red meat to fish is not only healthier as a dietary choice, it's environmentally friendly as well: Fish farming is generally "greener" than meat production.

4 Preserves Wild Stocks

Another advantage of aquaculture is its potential to reduce the strain on wild fisheries and native fish stocks. The more fish farming meets our needs, the less incentive there is to purchase wild-caught fish. That in turn reduces the temptation to overfish and improves the likelihood that wild stocks can maintain a healthy population. Immature fish bred in captivity can even be used to re-establish species in places where they've been wiped out by overfishing. However, one frequent criticism of fish farms is that they're not always efficient providers of dietary protein. Some operations rely on wild-caught "trash" fish or bait fish for much of their feed, meaning it's quite possible for the fish to consume more protein than they produce.

5 Risk to Wild Stocks

Unfortunately, fish farming also poses a risk to wild fish populations. Open-pen fish farms concentrate the creatures at unnaturally high levels, increasing waste and the risk of disease, just as many land-based hog and chicken farms do. This poses a threat to wild fish, which can be infected. Inland fresh-water systems can be just as harmful if they're located in a lake or river with its own wild species. Land-based systems that return used water to the local watershed also pose some risk. Escaped fish from these pens can become invasive, as fast-growing carp and tilapia do inland or farmed Atlantic salmon do on the West Coast.

6 Fish Farming as Entrepreneurial Opportunity

One additional advantage of fish farming is that it represents an opportunity from which entrepreneurs almost anywhere can benefit. Farms can be situated anywhere from open coastlines to a farmer's "back 40" to a shuttered factory in a Rust Belt city. Startup costs can be surprisingly low for a small operation, largely a matter of choosing the right species to cultivate and providing a suitable environment. Salmon, trout, catfish, tilapia, shrimp and crawfish are all common options. Some operators maximize their productivity through composite fish culture, which is raising a combination of compatible, noncompetitive species in the same bodies of water. This gives you more variety in your product line and more fish to sell at little additional cost.

● How economic Impact to fish and cotton farming industries

The social science of economics began as a branch of philosophy, but emerged as a separate discipline in the late 18th century after the publication of Adam Smith's landmark work, "The Wealth of Nations." Since then, economics has provided a scientific approach to understanding the ways in which families, firms and entire societies allocate resources to satisfy their needs and wants. People live in a world of scarcity in which all resources—time, money, land and others—are finite. Because people do not have unlimited resources, they must allocate their time, money and other resources in a way that will achieve as many of their needs and wants as possible. For example, consumers want to obtain maximum value for their money, and businesses want to maximize profits subject to their existing capacity for production. Economics provides a systematic way to study production, consumption and resource allocation.

Throughout history, people have dealt with issues of resource allocation; often human survival depended on it. The concept of an economy did not develop until the Middle Ages, although markets and trade have existed since ancient times. Until the era of the Enlightenment in the 18th century, economics was not a discipline of its own, but a branch of philosophy, which also examined political, ethical and religious issues.Just as biologists and chemists apply scientific methods to understand questions involving biological and chemical phenomena, economists employ scientific methods, including hypothesis testing and quantitative analysis, to understand and explain economic phenomena. Why apartment rents are so much higher in New York City than in Austin, Texas; how government monetary policy will affect retail prices; what factors affect average wages in different countries—these and other questions involve economic phenomena. As a science, economics strives to provide answers and explanations.

Hence, economics plays an important role in the analysis and formulation of government policy. Just as consumers want maximum value for their money, politicians and taxpayers want to maximize the value of their taxes and other government resources at the lowest cost. Economists have an important voice in the policy arena, helping identify the types of policies that maximize benefits at the least cost to the public.As a scientific approach to policy, economics not only informs the debate over issues related to taxation, government spending and economic policies; it also applies to the full range of public policy issues, including health care, defense, education, energy and the environment.

Catfish Farming How Bring Profit

If one fish farmer or cotton farmer is looking for a decisive argument in favor of aquaculture, simple economics can provide one. The U.S. imports over 90 percent of its seafood, creating a yearly trade deficit that the USDA's Agricultural Research Service estimated at $14 billion as of January 2018. When you combine that economic impact with a fish farm's ability to fit in almost anywhere, the potential is clear: Fish or cotton farming can produce economic growth in places where jobs are sorely needed. Managing a fish or cotton farm sustainably can help reduce its disadvantages and increase its advantages. For conventional open-pen operators, for example, that can mean reducing the populations of fish or cotton in each pen to cut down on waste and reduce the need for medications. On land, fish or cotton farmers can opt for recirculating aquaculture systems that filter and reuse the same water constantly, isolating the farmed fish from local waterways and minimizing the risk that they'll escape and become invasive. An especially appealing option is aquaponics, a method of growing vegetable crops such as herbs, lettuce and tomatoes hydroponically with the same water that supports the fish. Waste from the fish fertilizes the plants, which in turn helps filter the water and keeps the fish healthy.

Aquaculture dates back thousands of years ago and is now a rapidly expanding business practice in the United States. Operating a catfish farm, for example, requires a precise and well-executed business plan. Farm operators must raise large amounts of capital to even begin a small fish-farming practice. There are, however, many benefits to fish farming over cattle or chicken farming, and savvy business considerations can help you how to profit in the world of farming catfish. For example, invest in a large farm. Large farms, on one hand, demand more acreage, thus costing more money. A farm costing $5,000 per acre multiplied by 90 acres equals $450,000 in the initial investment of the pond property alone. Building a large farm, however, allows you to sell more fish at one time — substantially increasing profit margins over smaller farms. Moreover, larger farms can export more easily to international markets — such as Asia — where fish is widely consumed. Design fish farm in a location with moderate temperatures and geography. Climates with excessive rain or snow can damage fish farming with flooding or freezing water. Choosing a geographical location away from areas where fault lines, tornadoes or hurricanes can result in annual natural disasters is also wise for the preservation of fish farm.Sell fishes in direct sales. Selling catfish direct to market eliminates the costs of unnecessary business entities raising the cost and taking a cut of the profits before the product reaches the consumer. Direct sales to a processing factory — which then sells directly to the public — reduce the need for dealing with grocery store chains or other costly business outlets. Using direct sales is a way to keep consumer prices down, maintain the freshness in fish and sell more of the product at one time.

● Pros and Cons of Biotechnology in Agriculture

If most people had to list the disadvantages of biotechnology, agricultural uses would rank high. Just look at how many foods proudly advertise as having no genetically modified ingredients. What are the advantages and disadvantages of biotechnology in agriculture?

Consider the pros of biotechnology, they may include:

Genetically engineering crops can make them resistant to disease and insect attacks. Inserting genes that make crops immune to herbicide allows farmers to eliminate weeds without hurting crops. There's less need to till the soil to kill weeds, which reduces erosion. Plants can produce toxic chemicals that kill off insect predators. Genetic engineering can make plants produce more food or improve their nutritional profile. Biotechnology can keep plant foods shelf-stable for longer periods.

Consider the cons of biotechnology they may include:

As farmers use herbicides more regularly, it accelerates the development of immunity in weeds. Genetically modified organisms are covered by patents. Farmers who replant seeds from a patented crop as they would with ordinary plants have faced lawsuits. Relying on GMOs reduces the natural genetic diversity found in agriculture. If, say, all corn or soybeans have the same genetic profile, there's a greater chance of some fungus or parasite wiping out the entire national crop. GMO seed is more expensive, though it can also lead to greater profits from a larger yield.

Risks of Biotechnology in Humans

Many people are uneasy about having products from GMOs in their food. Genetic engineering in human beings raises even more concern about the negative aspects of biotechnology. Monstrous experiments on humans have been a staple of horror movies, and for many people, the real thing is equally as troubling.

Many diseases stem from genetic problems, so treating them genetically can save or transform lives. This is effective if there's a single genetic issue that's easy to identify and treat. It's possible that eventually, we will be able to enhance human beings: stronger hearts, greater intelligence, more disease resistance. Much of our bodies and health aren't the product of single genes but complex interactions. It's entirely possible that in trying to improve ourselves, we'll create unwanted, disastrous side effects.

Some genetic diseases aren't as simple to treat as fixing one rogue gene. There are serious ethical issues when science experiments on humans. If we're altering genes to "improve" people, does that raise different ethical questions from altering genes to fix verifiable problems? Can we regulate human biotechnological treatments to gain benefits while restricting abuse?

All of above biotechnology technology whether it ought to apply to any agriculture industry to bring advantages and disadvantges, any farmers or farming economists or agricultural scientists must need to evaluate whether what future negative or positive influences human will face.

CHAPTER II

How developing countries develop farming industry

● How India land supply shortage may influence India farming industry economic development

We know how agriculture contributes to economic development and then how industry contributes towards development. However, the issue of choice of one sector over the other remains unresolved as far as economic policy is concerned. Industry which is, no doubt, important, will not progress unless agriculture is sound, stable, and progressive. Because of this interdependence these sectors are complementary, and not competitive. In the development of an underdeveloped economy, there is as such no conflict between agricultural and industrial development.

Hence, interdependence between agriculture and industry becomes strengthened through various linkages generated in these two sectors. The three most important linkages are : production linkages, demand linkages, and saving-investment linkages.Production linkages arise from the interdependence between agriculture and industry through the use of productive inputs. Agriculture draws some raw materials, like chemical fertilisers, pesticides, electric power, agricultural machinery and implements, etc., from the industry. Agriculture is also dependent on industry for the supply of materials for building up social and economic overheads in the agricultural sector. Further, many raw materials and inputs used in industrial production, e.g., cotton, jute, sugarcane, tobacco, etc., is supplied by the agricultural sector.

Demand linkages between the two sectors suggest that demand for one sector's product pulls demand for another sector in an upward direction. Urbanisation and industrialisation are synonymous. Under the impact of Green Revolution, agriculturists now experience rising rural incomes which has brought a change in the pattern of tastes and preferences of rural people. Increased rural income has resulted in an entry of industrial consumer goods, like TV, refrigerator, modem, car, footwear, refined sugar, edible oils, motorbikes, etc. In the urban areas, we see some sort of demand saturation of some of these products of consumer goods industries. The impact of rising urban incomes and industrialisation has a favourable impact on the demand for food, vegetables, fruits, various raw materials produced in the agricultural sector. It has been an article of faith in India that the demand stimulus for industrial expansion would likely come mainly from agriculture with low social and economic costs.

Finally, there is a savings-investment linkage between these two sectors. A self-reliant agriculture capable of exporting surplus food-grains helps in saving scarce foreign exchange resources of the country. Now these resources can be better utilised for importing capital goods and crucial raw materials needed for industrialisation effort. As agricultural production and productivity rises above the subsistence requirement, the volume of marketable surplus increases which provides sinews of industrialisation, particularly in the rural sector. Again, the rising volume of savings and capital formation consequent upon rising farm incomes give strong stimulus to demand for manufactured goods.

Investment in one sector pulls investment of other sectors up thereby accelerating overall growth rate of the economy. Similarly, the rise in non-farm incomes leads to an increase in the demand for various agricultural products. In the process, agricultural sector becomes diversified, modernised. Most importantly, the relative terms of trade between the two sectors affect the flow of resources from one to another sector. Terms of trade will improve for agricultural sector if over a period of time the prices of agricultural commodities move at a higher rate than the prices of manufactured articles. Thus, the terms of trade favouring agriculture results in an increased real income and hence, increased private saving and investment. The relative terms of trade also influence government saving and investment in these two sectors.If technological change is made in the primary sector there will be more surplus and, hence, more output in the industrial sector.

In the end, we must say a few words about the problem of inter-sectoral resource allocation. To begin with, it is almost impossible to make an optimum balance between these two sectors. In many of the developing countries, agriculture no longer enjoys a pride of place, for some obvious reasons. Neo-liberal era has seen the over-emphasis on the urban, industrial sector. That is why agricultural land is now being forcibly taken away for industrial development, infrastructural developments, and so on. Against this backdrop, farmers of these economies have been shifting their attention from the agricultural sector towards non- agricultural activities. How far these two sectors will complement each other, and to what degree, is an important issue. Indeed, the failure on the agriculture front is of tern attributed to faulty agricultural policy in many developing countries, including India. So,

India is one good farming industry needing developing country example, any India fish and corn , furit , wheat, rice and meat farmers must need to concern how to use land natural resource for their farming development in order to avoid farming lands shorage challenge to influence India farming industry economic development.

● The Relationship between Economic Growth and Agricultural Growth To China

What is agricultural industry policy to future China ? China is number one in Agriculture. China ranks first in worldwide farm output, primarily producing rice, wheat, potatoes, tomato, sorghum, peanuts, tea, millet, barley, cotton, oilseed, corn and soybeans. The development of farming over the course of China's history has played a key role in supporting the growth of what is now the largest population in the world. Analysis of stone tools by Professor Liu Li and others has shown that hunter-gatherers 23,000–19,500 years ago ground wild plants with the same tools that would later be used for millet and rice.

What is China Farming method improvements ? Due to China's status as a developing country and its severe shortage of arable land, farming in China has always been very labor-intensive. However, throughout its history, various methods have been developed or imported that enabled greater farming production and efficiency. They also utilized the seed drill to help improve on row farming. For agricultural purposes the Chinese had invented the hydraulic-powered trip hammer by the 1st century BC. Although it found other purposes, its main function was to pound, decorticate, and polish grain that otherwise would have been done manually. The Chinese also innovated the square-pallet chain pump by the 1st century AD, powered by a waterwheel or oxen pulling on a system of mechanical wheels. Although the chain pump found use in public works of providing water for urban and palatial pipe systems, it was used largely to lift water from a lower to higher elevation in filling irrigation canals and channels for farmland.

Since 1994, the government has instituted a number of policy changes aimed at limiting grain importation and increasing economic stability. Among these policy changes was the artificial increase of grain prices above market levels. This has led to increased grain production, while placing the heavy burden of maintaining these prices on the government. In 1995, the "Governor's Grain Bag Responsibility System" was instituted, holding provincial governors responsible for balancing grain supply and demand and stabilizing grain prices in their provinces. Later, in 1997, the "Four Separations and One Perfection" program was implemented to relieve some of the monetary burdens placed on the government by its grain policy. As China continues to industrialize, vast swaths of agricultural land is being converted into industrial land. Farmers displaced by such urban expansion often become migrant labor for factories, but other farmers feel disenfranchised and cheated by the encroachment of industry and the growing disparity between urban and rural wealth and income.

The most recent innovation in Chinese agriculture is a push into organic agriculture. This rapid embrace of organic farming simultaneously serves multiple purposes, including food safety, health benefits, export opportunities, and, by providing price premiums for the produce of rural communities, the adoption of organics can help stem the migration of rural workers to the cities.In the mid-1990s China became a net importer of grain, since its unsustainable practises of groundwater mining has effectively removed considerable land from productive agricultural use. Due to China's status as a developing country and its severe shortage of arable land, farming in China has always been very labor-intensive. However, throughout its history, various methods have been developed or imported that enabled greater farming production and efficiency. They also utilized the seed drill to help improve on row farming.

However, China's agricultural productivity grew rapidly following the implementation of a series of economic reforms since 1978. Reforms led to more efficient resource allocation. China also began to disseminate new technologies (including improved seed varieties and animal breeds) and encourage mechanization. These "agricultural modernization" efforts laid a broad foundation for improved agricultural productivity. But evidence suggests that this growth may not continue into the future. With about 20 percent of the world's population, 6.5 percent of its land area, and rising living standards, China's ability to improve farm productivity will have a direct bearing on global food markets. China is already the leading importer of soybeans and cotton and has recently emerged as an importer of other major commodities, including corn, pork, wheat, and rice. A slowdown in productivity growth could bring further demand for imports.

During 1985-2007, China's agricultural output growth (in real terms) averaged 5.1 percent annually. Two developments underlie this growth: greater use of inputs and growth in what economists call "total factor productivity" (TFP), or the ability to produce more output from each unit of input. TFP growth contributed 2.7 percentage points to the growth in China's agricultural output while rising use of inputs contributed 2.4 percentage points. The mix of inputs changed as use of intermediate goods (including energy, pesticides, fertilizer, seed, feed, and other materials) grew 6.4 percent annually, offsetting declines in the use of labor and land. China's roughly equal reliance on increased input use and TFP contrasts with the recent experience of developed countries where TFP accounts for nearly all growth in agricultural output. For example, annual growth in U.S. agricultural TFP contributed 1.22 percentage points while input growth contributed 0.03 percentage points to output growth over 1985-2007. Future China farming productivities may include below several aspects:

1 Crop distribution

Although China's agricultural output is the largest in the world, only 10% of its total land area can be cultivated. China's arable land, which represents 10% of the total arable land in the world, supports over 20% of the world's population.[23] Of this approximately 1.4 million square kilometers of arable land, only about 1.2% (116,580 square kilometers) permanently supports crops and 525,800 square kilometers are irrigated.[citation needed] The land is divided into approximately 200 million households, with an average land allocation of just 0.65 hectares, China is the leading producer of cotton, which is grown throughout, but especially in the areas of the North China Plain, the Yangtze river delta, the middle Yangtze valley, and the Xinjiang Uygur Autonomous Region. Other fiber crops include ramie, flax, jute, and hemp. Sericulture, the practice of silkworm raising, is also practiced in central and southern China.

2 Livestock

China has a large livestock population, with pigs and fowls

being the most common. China's pig population and pork production mainly lie along the Yangtze River. In 2011, Sichuan province had 51 million pigs (11% of China's total supply).[30] In rural western China, sheep, goats, and camels are raised by nomadic herders.[31] In Tibet, yaks are raised as a source of food, fuel, and shelter. Cattle, water buffalo, horses, mules, and donkeys are also raised in China, and dairy has recently been encouraged by the government, even though approximately 92.3% of the adult population is affected by some level of lactose intolerance. As demand for gourmet foods grows, production of more exotic meats increases as well. Based on survey data from 684 Chinese turtle farms (less than half of the all 1,499 officially registered turtle farms in the year of the survey, 2002), they sold over 92,000 tons of turtles (around 128 million animals) per year; this is thought to correspond to the industrial total of over 300 million turtles per year. Increased incomes and increased demand for meat, especially pork, has resulted in demand for improved breeds of livestock, breeding stock imported particularly from the United States. Some of these breeds are adapted to factory farming.

3 Fishing

China accounts for about one-third of the total fish production of the world. Aquaculture, the breeding of fish in ponds and lakes, accounts for more than half of its output. The principal aquaculture-producing regions are close to urban markets in the middle and lower Yangtze valley and the Zhu Jiang delta.

● What risks China will encounter to farming industry

All of China's regions have experienced strong growth in agricultural production since the mid-1980s fueled by both input and TFP growth, but the relative contribution of these two factors differs by region. Provinces with the most rapid TFP growth include a mix of coastal regions that led China's economic development and several western provinces. Most northeastern and northern provinces exhibited more input growth. Although the growing economy has pulled labor and land away from farming, the development of China's nonfarm sectors may have benefited farming by generating funds for investment in public infrastructure, science, and technology. Relaxed restrictions on foreign trade and investment may also have enhanced agricultural productivity by improving access to new technology and new markets.

However, the rapid growth in the past few decades may not have been sustained in recent years. Annual TFP growth peaked during 1996-2000 at 5.1 percent before slowing to 3.2 percent in 2000-2005. It then declined by 3.7 percent per year in 2005-07. The significance of this slowdown remains unclear. It may reflect a turning point in China's agricultural productivity growth, in which case gains from earlier reforms and technology transfers from developed countries have been exhausted. Alternatively, it may simply be the effect of transitory events such as animal disease epidemics or discrepancies in data. As urbanization draws more labor and land from agriculture and accelerates changes in food consumption, the capacity to reestablish positive agricultural TFP growth is important to China's future. So, China needs to concerns below several aspects to raise itself farming industry competitive position to global farming competitive market.

1) Finance is emerging as a major driver of sustainability. Government policy and consumer preferences can certainly shift corporate behaviour, as tariffs on soy have shown. And most consumer-facing businesses are adapting

to their customers' preferences for more sustainability.

2) Innovation will be part of any solution.

While the public sector has limited funding resources, private investment and capability could play an instrumental role in achieving sustainable agricultural development goals. But current levels are not enough to meet global food security challenges in the long term. Private investors remain reluctant to invest in sustainable agriculture because of the perceived uncertainties and high risks. Furthermore, conventional financing models have their limits, particularly in developing countries where most of the growth in food demand and production will come from. China need more innovative financing in which public and private sectors can work together, to create the necessary policy and investment environment for private finance in sustainable farming. China also should look at the renewable energy sector for new ideas, where public-private partnerships (PPPs) have successfully delivered mechanisms for pooling public and private financing and risk mitigation. Chinese people may not like change, but they like innovation. People don't like to give things up, but they like to have new options. Innovation is the answer. It is essential to change.

3) Success depends on collaboration. Bringing people on board is a must. To identify a solution is much easier than to implement it. In theory, everybody wants a more sustainable food system. But not everybody wants or is able to pay the price. That's why sustainable change requires us to bring on board all those who are affected. In order to achieve a sustainable food chain, farmers and producers may need further incentives. China's sizeable Grain for Green project offered grains, tax and other encouragements so that farmers would protect, instead of

clear, their forested slopes. And agribusinesses will be wise to adopt the same principle. Sustainable farming will only be possible if farmers are on board.

4) Success requires solutions at scale and China is well-placed to deliver them.

The urgency of our biodiversity and climate crises means that we need to have solutions in place right now. And these solutions need to be at scale. The sustainability-linked loan mentioned above is not the first in the agricultural trading sector, but it is the largest so far. It demonstrates our intention to join hands with others in our industry and to contribute to sustainable growth in the global agriculture sector. That is part of the Chinese dream.

Hence, all of above technological innovation is needed to developed to China future farm industry, if it still hope to raise farming competitive position in global farming market.

● What factors influence US farming development

In farming economic view, in general, these factors will influence any countries farming industry developement. They may include: Human factors that influence agricultural use include: Population size leads to larger areas of cultivation and competitio for land. Farming techniques. Final destination of production. Globalisation . Agricultural policies. Environmental policies aim to protect the environment and guarantee safe, healthy food. Social and economic factors. These are human factors and include labour, capital, technology, markets and government (political). These are physical factors and include climate, relief and soil. Temperature (minimum 6°C for crops to grow) and rainfall (at least 250mm to 500mm) influence the types of crops that can be grown, e.g. hot, wet tropical areas favour rice, while cooler, drier areas favour wheat.

Although farming is one of the world's oldest professions, modern farming is affected by uniquely modern economic factors. Farmers today compete in a complex economic environment where customers choose from produce grown all over the world and governments provide financial incentives for the production of certain crops rather than others. Such as US is one developed country, whether what are the main factors to influence its farming industry development. I shall indicate these main factors as below:

The history of agriculture in the United States covers the period from the first English settlers to the present day. In Colonial America, agriculture was the primary livelihood for 90% of the population, and most towns were shipping points for the export of agricultural products. Most farms were geared toward subsistence production for family use. The rapid growth of population and the expansion of the frontier opened up large numbers of new farms, and clearing the land was a major preoccupation of farmers. After 1800, cotton became the chief crop in southern plantations, and the chief American export. After 1840, industrialization and urbanization opened up lucrative domestic markets. The number of farms grew from 1.4 million in 1850, to 4.0 million in 1880, and 6.4 million in 1910; then started to fall, dropping to 5.6 million in 1950 and 2.2 million in 2008.

Nowadays, US farming productivities may include :

Arable farming , it means growing of cereals, vegetables and animal feeds. Flat relief; fertile well-drained soils; warm summers; rainfall – under 650mm (some in growing season); winter frosts to break up soil and kill pestsPhysical factors Flat relief; fertile well-drained soils; warm summers; rainfall – under 650mm (some in growing season); winter frosts to break up soil and kill pests as well as Human factors. Large market in south east; good transport networks; benefits from US government subsidies and intervention price, they can influence US arable farming success.

Dairying, Rearing of cattle for milk. Hill sheep farming, sheep rearing for meat .Physical factors, Gentle relief; fertile soils; high rainfall for grass growth; mild winters (over 6°C).Human factors. Access to large markets; milk subsidies up to the 1980s when quotas introduce, they can influence US dairying development success.

Hill sheep farming.Wool and Market gardening, growing fruit, vegetables and flowers. Physical factors, High, steep relief; thin infertile soils; high rainfall (over 1000mm); low temperatures unsuitable for crops. Human factors, Remote from large markets; limited labour; EU subsidies and grants, they may influence hill sheep farming success.

Market gardening includes Growing fruit, vegetables and flowers. Physical factors, Long hours of sunshine; most other factors are controlled. Human factors, Access to motorways and airports; large labour and capital input. They may influence marketing gardening success.

There are these main factors still influence US future agricultural industry development as below:

On Human Factors aspect, it may include: Labour: All farms need either human labour or machinery to do the work. Some farm types use very little labour, e.g. sheep farming. Others require a large labour force, e.g. rice farming in India. Market: This is the customer who buys farm produce. Farmers need to sell their crops and animals to make a profit. Perishable crops such as soft fruits fetch a high price, but need to be grown with a short travelling distance of the market. Finance: Profits are used to pay the wages and to re-invest in the farm, e.g. buying seeds, fertiliser, machinery and animals. This is known as feedback within the farming system. Tradition: Farmers may have always farmed in a certain way and be unwilling to change. Politics: Government may provide subsidies and loans to encourage new farming practices but they may also place limits on production to prevent food surpluses, e.g. quotas and set-aside in the European Union.

On Physical Factors aspect, it may include: Climate: Temperature – a minimum temperature of 6°C is needed for crops to grow. The growing season is the number of months the temperature is over 6°C. Different crops need a different growing season, e.g. wheat needs 90 days. Rainfall – all crops and animals need water. Relief: Temperatures decrease by 1>°C every 160 metres vertical height. Uplands are more exposed to wind and rain. Steep slopes also cause thin soils and limit the use of machinery. Lowland areas are more easily farmed. Soils: Crops grow best on deep, fertile, free-draining soils, e.g. the brown earths found in lowland Britain. Less fertile soils prone to water logging are best used for pastoral farming. Geography Aspect: The direction a slope faces. South-facing slopes are best for growing crops.

Hence, environment and human, e.g. farmers, government, farming scientists etc. both will be main factors to influence US future farming industry development.

CHAPTER III

How farming influences developing and developed countries economic development

● How Agriculture Contributes to Economic Development ?

To explain why and how agriculture can influence economic development. We need to know whether agriculture role is important to our societies. Agriculture has always played a pivotal role in shaping the economy of countries. Since it fulfills the basic necessities of the people, all nations across the globe make special provision to improve the productivity. Even the ancient civilization has given it due importance. The agriculture sector not only provides food but also a means of employment to millions. It contributes to resolving sociopolitical issues and building a civilized society. Countries where the real capital income is less, more emphasis is given on developing the agricultural sector and its related industries since it can become the driving force to boost the economy. Whether under developing or developed, agriculture is still the basic occupation of the world.

I feel that role of agriculture may be explained as: With the discovery of agriculture, the hunter-gatherer community found a source for food, settling down at one place, and reduce hunting. The agricultural revolution changed the way the farming sector would impact the overall economy of a country. The agricultural development assisted greatly for industrialization in countries like U.S. and Japan as evident from the significant progress made by them. As a result, it became clear to the underdeveloped and developing countries that instead of putting limitations on a particular sector, the industrial and agricultural industries must co-exist for contributing to the development of the nation. The agricultural industry plays a big role in driving an economy being a major source of raw materials. It not increases the employment ratio, but also strengthens the purchasing power of the people. This sector can also help individuals for playing an instrumental role in country's foreign exports, and providing job opportunities for all types of skills. So, agriculture may create new jobs, e.g. supermarket, farming, fishing, restaurant, food wholeseller, food manufacture. Any related food activities industries may be influenced to creat any jobs changes by agricultural development.

Ways May Agriculture Boosts a Country's Economy, it may includes these several ways. Whether it is a developed country or a developing one, agriculture forms an important sector in improving GDP, which is important to determine the economic performance of a nation For the industries which are agro-based, it is the backbone of their products as major raw materials are obtained from the farm. The agricultural industry plays a significant role in boosting the national income in various ways such as:

1 Improving employment ratio

The agriculture sector and livestock industry are interlinked. Together, they create many job opportunities for the population. While the agriculture sector employs people for agricultural production, the livestock industry does it for producing and selling animal products. Since both these industries need to function through a chain of ancillary support such as warehouse and logistics, it helps in generating employment for the people.

2 Promotes infrastructure creation

When the focus is shifted towards development of agriculture, naturally, it boosts the small-scale industries situated in the vicinity of that area. As it involves a lot of operations, it would eventually mean the development of roads, storehouses, packaging units, and transportation services thus adding to the development of new infrastructure, when any countries food wholesalers need to deliver any foods to local or overseas by air planes, ships, lorries , railways etc. transport tools. So, it encourage non food direct relationship industries development in the world.

3 Helps to supply raw materials

Agriculture helps to produce raw materials that are required by other industries. Processing of these raw materials helps in manufacturing products for several uses. If the supply of materials is not as per the demand, then it can affect the entire supply chain thereby impacting the economyAs a result, the nation's economic turnover might take a hit thus adding to more expenses for the people.

4 Generates a source of foreign exchange for the country

Most of the primary products that are required in industries are obtained from the agricultural sector. For instance, the refined quality cotton dresses which you purchase from the mall get their basic material from the farm. When the raw material is available in abundance, the country can become a primary exporter of the products and generate a good income. As the international market is very dynamic and since the price of raw material is constantly fluctuating, the developing countries have now started focusing on the export of manufactured foods to increase the percentage of foreign income.

5 Bringing non -food primary sectors development chance

By providing food and raw material to non-agricultural sectors of the economy, by creating demand for goods produced in non-agricultural sectors, by the rural people on the strength of the purchasing power, earned by them on selling the marketable surplus, by providing investable surplus in the form of savings and taxes to be invested in non-agricultural sector, by earning valuable foreign exchange through the export of agricultural products,

On conclusion, the agricultural sector can assist to contribute significantly in generating capital income for a country in many ways. For example, when there is a surplus demand for the raw materials, it will, in turn, lead to the production of more goods supporting industrialization and increasing employment. Hence, when a country focuses on making advancements in the agricultural sector, it is, in turn, contributing to its own economic development by starting to address the problems at the root level. Giving significance to the issues at the base level can help to cut down the obstacles in the later stages, and also boost income for an economy.

● What is the main Role of Agriculture in Economic Development?

The agriculture sector is the backbone of an economy which provides the basic ingredients to mankind and now raw material for industrialisation. So, I believe that agriculture and industrialisation development must have direct relationship to bring both development. If the country's agriculture can develop better, then its industrialisation can also develop better. The reasons may include as below:

1. Contribution to National Income:

The lessons drawn from the economic history of many advanced countries tell us that agricultural prosperity contributed considerably in fostering economic advancement. It is correctly observed that, "The leading industrialized countries of today were once predominantly agricultural while the developing economies still have the dominance of agriculture and it largely contributes to the national income. In India, still 28% of national income comes from this sector.

2. Source of Food Supply:

Agriculture is the basic source of food supply of all the countries of the world—whether underdeveloped, developing or even developed. Due to heavy pressure of population in underdeveloped and developing countries and its rapid increase, the demand for food is increasing at a fast rate. If agriculture fails to meet the rising demand of food products, it is found to affect adversely the growth rate of the economy. Raising supply of food by agricultural sector has, therefore, great importance for economic growth of a country.

3. Pre-Requisite for Raw Material:

Agricultural advancement is necessary for improving the supply of raw materials for the agro-based industries especially in developing countries. The shortage of agricultural goods has its impact upon on industrial production and a consequent increase in the general price level. It will impede the growth of the country's economy. The flour mills, rice shellers, oil & dal mills, bread, meat, milk products sugar factories, wineries, jute mills, textile mills and numerous other industries are based on agricultural products.

4. Provision of Surplus:

The progress in agricultural sector provides surplus for increasing the exports of agricultural products. In the earlier stages of development, an increase in the exports earning is more desirable because of the greater strains on the foreign exchange situation needed for the financing of imports of basic and essential capital goods.

5. Shift of Manpower:

Initially, agriculture absorbs a large quantity of labour force. In India still about 62% labour is absorbed in this sector. Agricultural progress permits the shift of manpower from agricultural to non-agricultural sector. In the initial stages, the diversion of labour from agricultural to non-agricultural sector is more important from the point of view of economic development as it eases the burden of surplus labour force over the limited land. Thus, the release of surplus manpower from the agricultural sector is necessary for the progress of agricultural sector and for expanding the non-agricultural sector.

6. Creation of Infrastructure:

The development of agriculture requires roads, market yards, storage, transportation railways, postal services and many others for an infrastructure creating demand for industrial products and the development of commercial sector.

7. Relief from Shortage of Capital:

The development of agricultural sector has minimized the burden of several developed countries who were facing the shortage of foreign capital. If foreign capital is available with the 'strings' attached to it, it will create another significant problem. Agriculture sector requires less capital for its development thus it minimizes growth problem of foreign capital.

8. Helpful to Reduce Inequality:

In a country which is predominantly agricultural and overpopulated, there is greater inequality of income between the rural and urban areas of the country. To reduce this inequality of income, it is necessary to accord higher priority to agriculture. The prosperity of agriculture would raise the income of the majority of the rural population and thus the disparity in income may be reduced to a certain extent. Such as India and China developing countries , agricultural development must help to reduce their people income inequality.

9. Based on Democratic Notions:

If the agricultural sector does not grow at a faster rate, it may result in the growing discontentment amongst the masses which is never healthy for the smooth running of democratic governments. For economic development, it is necessary to minimize political as well as social tensions. In case the majority of the people have to be kindled with the hopes of prosperity, this can be attained with the help of agricultural progress. Thus development of agriculture sector is also relevant on political and social grounds.

10. Create Effective Demand:

The development of agricultural sector would tend to increase the purchasing power of agriculturists which will help the growth of the non-agricultural sector of the country. It will provide a market for increased production. In underdeveloped countries, it is well known that the majority of people depend upon agriculture and it is they who must be able to afford to consume the goods produced. Therefore, it will be helpful in stimulating the growth of the non- agricultural sector. Similarly improvement in the productivity of cash crops may pave the way for the promotion of exchange economy which may help the growth of non-agricultural sector. Purchase of industrial products such as pesticides, farm machinery etc. also provide boost to industrial dead out.

11. Helpful in prolonging Economic Depression:
During depression, industrial production can be stopped or reduced but agricultural production continues as it produces basic necessities of life. Thus it continues to create effective demand even during adverse conditions of the economy.

12. Source of Foreign Exchange for the Country:
Most of the developing countries of the world are exporters of primary products, such as India and China. These products contribute 60 to 70 per cent of their total export earning. Thus, the capacity to import capital goods and machinery for industrial development depends crucially on the export earning of the agriculture sector. If exports of agricultural goods fail to increase at a sufficiently high rate, these countries are forced to incur heavy deficit in the balance of payments resulting in a serious foreign exchange problem. However, primary goods face declining prices in international market and the prospects of increasing export earnings through them are limited. Due to this, large developing countries like India (having potentialities of industrial development) are trying to diversify their production structure and promote the exports of manufactured goods even though this requires the adoption of protective measures in the initial period of planning.

13. Contribution to Capital Formation:
Underdeveloped and developing countries need huge amount of capital for its economic development. In the initial stages of economic development, it is agriculture that constitutes a significant source of capital formation. Such as
(i) agricultural taxation,
(ii) export of agricultural products,

(iii) collection of agricultural products at low prices by the government and selling it at higher prices. This method is adopted by Russia and China,

(iv) labour in disguised unemployment, largely confined to agriculture, is viewed as a source of investible surplus,

(v) transfer of labour and capital from farm to non-farm activities etc.

14. Employment Opportunities for Rural People:
Agriculture provides employment opportunities for rural people on a large scale in underdeveloped and developing countries. It is an important source of livelihood. Generally, landless workers and marginal farmers are engaged in non-agricultural jobs like handicrafts, furniture, textiles, leather, metal work, processing industries, and in other service sectors. These rural units fulfill merely local demands. In India about 70.6% of total labour force depends upon agriculture. So, India and China many rural people have huge job chance , when themselve faming industry can be developed technological agricultural development in success.

15. Improving Rural Welfare:
It is time that rural economy depends on agriculture and allied occupations in an underdeveloped country. The rising agricultural surplus caused by increasing agricultural production and productivity tends to improve social welfare, particularly in rural areas. The living standard of rural masses rises and they start consuming nutritious diet including eggs, milk, ghee and fruits. They lead a comfortable life having all modern amenities—a better house, motor-cycle, radio, television and use of better clothes.

16. Extension of Market for Industrial Output:
As a result of agricultural progress, there will be extension

of market for industrial products. Increase in agricultural productivity leads to increase in the income of rural population which is turn leads to more demand for industrial products, thus development of industrial sector. So, any agricultural productive machine, even artificial intelligent agricultural productive machine will be increased to any countries farmers' needs when they need to apply these farming machines to help them to raise crop productivities in short time , reducing workers numbers , reduces farming expenditures, short food delivery time. So, farming industrial tools invention is needed rapidly.

● The Influence of Agriculture On The Socio-Economic Development of Regions

How agriculture can influence to any countries' socio economic development of regions. For example, how China 's India's and US's rural regions can bring socio economic development of rural regions. The development of the field of agriculture has a positive impact on many people within the society. Rural and vulnerable groups and regions are influenced the most. Firstly, we must need to know whether what positive influences will bring to influence any countries' regions socio-economy, such as: The role of agriculture in food security. Population growth and demand for labor. The impact of agriculture in developing countries. Ecological challenges for the field of agriculture. All of these are main factors to impact any countries' regions socio economic development by agriculture development, when US, India and China countries can develop themselve agricultural industires of regions.

The majority of poor people and vulnerable societal groups live in rural regions. According to the study conducted by the US department of agriculture, poop people depend on agriculture when it comes to their livelihood. Therefore, it becomes quite obvious why agriculture plays such a crucial role in reducing poverty. Apart from providing the most vulnerable groups with food, it also gives them jobs. As a result of that, the rapid development of agriculture in rural areas has a huge impact on the cost of food for poor consumers. Once that cost is stabilized and the most vulnerable citizens can secure a job, their position in the society changes for the better. When they have a steady job, they are able to live a more comfortable life and enjoy more benefits our society can offer. Taking into consideration the fact that the field of agriculture is one of the very few options to get a steady job in rural areas, making sure this field is supported by the government should always be a top priority. However, when US, India and China decide the regions to develop themselve farming industry, these factors will influence their regions to develop agricultural industry success, such as: How to make farming more sustainable.How to deal with extreme weather conditions as well as how to improve the quality of soil on the regions.

However, if these countries' agricultural regions cannot come up with a more sustainable approach to agriculture, soon we will have no land to farm on. The latter is a very dire prospect which is the reason why it is time to get creative. For instance, urban framing is a great option. While rural areas remain focused on producing huge amounts of harvest (such as corn or wheat), people involved in urban farming projects can satisfy the need for fresh vegetables and greens in one part of the city. This way, both the consumers and the industry win.

There are numerous socio-cultural, economic, political, technological and infrastructural factors which also determine the agricultural land use, cropping patterns and agricultural processes. Of these factors, land tenancy, system of ownership, size of holdings, availability of labour and capital, religion, level of technological development, accessibility to the market, irrigation facilities, agricultural research and extension service, price incentives, government plans and international policies have a close impact on agricultural activities.

1. Land Tenancy:

Land tenure includes all forms of tenancy and also ownership in any form. Land tenancy and land tenure affect the agricultural operations and cropping patterns in many ways. The farmers and cultivators plan the agricultural activities and farm (fields) management keeping in mind their rights and possession duration on the land. In different communities of the world, the cultivators have different land tenancy rights. In the tribal societies of the shifting cultivators land belongs to the community and individuals are allowed only to grow crops along with other members of the community for a specific period. But among the sedentary farmers land belongs to individual farmers. In such societies it is believed that one who owns land he owns wealth.

The ownership and the length of time available for planning, development and management of arable land influence the decision making process of the cultivator. Depending on the nature of tenancy rights he decides the extent to which investment on land could be made. For example, if the cultivator is the sole owner of the land, he may install a tube well in his farm and may go for fencing and masonry irrigation channels. But a tenant farmer or a sharecropper will not go for the long term investment in the field as after a short period of occupancy he will have to vacate the land and the real owner may cultivate that piece of land either himself or may lease out to other cultivator. In fact, a farmer who has the right of ownership, he has the freedom to choose a system of production and investment which improves the quality of land and gives him increasing capacity to borrow money. The cropping patterns and farm management are also dependent on the duration of time for which the land is to remain under cultivation. For example, among the shifting cultivators (Jhumias of northeast India), the allotment of land to the cultivator is normally done for one or two years, depending on the fertility of the land.

The hilly terrain, the limited rights of the occupant and poor economic condition of the tillers hinder the development and efficient management of land. Since the land belongs to the community and not to the individuals, this type of land tenancy prevents the energetic, efficient and skilled individuals of the community to invest in the farm. Under such a system individuals are also unlikely to put much efforts or invest more money on the improvement of cultivated land as the field is allotted by the community for a short period. Under this type of land tenancy there is no incentive to individuals to improve the agricultural efficiency and productivity of the land. Contrary to this, a tenant having a lease for a longer period has considerable incentive to make his own improvements in drainage, irrigation channels, fencing and soil sustainability practices. Such leases are, however, rare. The tenancy system of short duration lease leads to insecurity for tenants. In India, the fear of landlords regaining control of farms has led to restrictions on long term letting. This has resulted into eleven months lease system. In the annual leasing system, however, very high rents are obtainable. In the short leasing system, it has been suggested that it enables a farmer to adopt his holding to his immediate needs but there is a strange temptation for a person who is working on the land only for one year to extract from the land as much as he can and put back the minimum. Consequently, the health of the soil due to unscientific rotation of crop is lost.

In India, at the time of independence (1947), there were two main tenure systems, i.e., the zamindari and the raiyatwari. These systems determined the relations between land on the one hand and the interested parties, the government, the owners and the cultivators, on the other. In the zamindari system, the land property rights were conferred upon persons who were avowedly non-cultivators but had sufficient influence in the region to collect land revenue from the cultivating peasantry. This was necessary at a time when the foreign government was not firmly established and direct control of land revenue and contact with the peasants was difficult. Owing to the zamindari tenure system, the real cultivators and tillers were exploited. They were, therefore, not interested in making investment in the land. Owner-cultivators who have a good deal of incentives to invest in land to improve the techniques of cultivation and to enhance productivity were discouraged. The tenant-cultivators in such a system face major disincentives like the fear of eviction, the insecurity of tenure, the rack-renting practice, the high rents and the inadequate surplus to invest.

In Southeast Asia, Latin America and parts of Southern Europe a system of land tenure known as 'metayage' is very widespread. In its simplest form it is a copartner ship between the owner who provides land, equipments, buildings, seeds, fertilizers and the metayer (cultivator) who provides labour and stock in return of a fixed share of the produce. The system sometimes involves pure sharecropping, i.e., there is no fixed rent, but the tenant cultivates the land and gives the owner a share, often 50 per cent of the agricultural produce.

In northern India, this system is known as 'Batai' This tenural system gives the tenant some protection from fluctuations in productions and crop prices and is usually preferable to fixed cash tenancies in which a tenant tends to fall progressively deeper into debts, whenever income from his crop falls below the outgoing rent. The traditional method of covering the deficit is by having recourse to a moneylender—a role used to be performed by the Jews in Europe, Greeks in the Middle East and the Bohras and Baniyas in India. In the rural areas of the developing countries, the moneylenders often charge exorbitant rates of interest and wield considerable power.

2. Size of Holdings and Fragmentation of Fields:

It is not only the land tenancy and the system of ownership which influence the agricultural and cropping patterns, the size of holdings and fragmentation of fields also have a close bearing on agricultural land use patterns and yields per unit area. In the densely populated areas of the developing countries the size of holdings is generally very small. The size of holding and the size of farm decide the degree of risk that a farm operator may bear. In general, larger the size of the farm, greater the capacity of the farmer to take the risk and vice versa. This, in turn, would affect the extent of specialization and also the nature of technology and equipment's (tractors, thrashers, harvesters, etc.) to be used.

In India, the average size of holding is very small. In fact, about 70 per cent of the total holdings are below one and a half hectares. The average standard size of holding that may give better agricultural returns cannot be maintained because of the fast growing rural population and the prevailing law of inheritance. The law of succession in the countries like India, Pakistan, Bangladesh and Sri Lanka results in the subdivision and fragmentation of holdings.

According to the law of inheritance in these countries, the property of the deceased is equally divided among the male heirs. Each son generally insists on having a share from each location and from each piece of land, resulting into further fragmentation of land. It is a wasteful and uneconomic method of land utilization in which improved agricultural practices cannot be adopted. The disadvantages of fragmentation of holdings are well known. It puts a large proportion of land outside the possibility of effective cultivation or economic development. The small fields are difficult to work with modern machinery and tractors etc.

n the opinion of agricultural economists, the fragmentation of holdings is a great obstacle and one of the major deterrents to economically viable cultivation. It results in wastage of land, labour and material inputs. It is responsible for increased overhead costs, including even the cost of production resulting in low returns from agriculture. The division of holdings may be socially justifiable but economically they are not viable.

3. Consolidation of Holdings and Operational Efficiency:
In order to overcome the disadvantages of fragmentation of holdings, consolidation of holdings has been done in many parts of the country. The advantages of consolidation of holdings are manifold. Important amongst them have been explained below. The fragmentation of holdings makes the efficient management and supervision of the farm operations difficult. It causes considerable waste of labour

of the cultivator and his plough cattle. Land consolidation makes it necessary for him to look after the crops and put up a fence around the holding.

It also enables the farmer to construct a farm house on the holding and shed for his cattle and thus exercise efficient supervision and management. The use of tractors and machinery also becomes possible in the case of substantial holdings. All these advantages are reflected in inputs cost and increase in production. The area wasted in embankments and boundaries in scattered holdings is released for cultivation after land consolidation. The farmer can take effective steps in the areas where soil erosion is a problem. Moreover, it helps in the development of better road linkages. The consolidation of holdings would, however, be fruitless if the advantages derived from the operations were to disappear as a result of the acts contrary to the purpose of consolidation leading to fragmentation of the consolidated properties.

Apart from solving the problems of consolidation of holdings, there must be a size of farm below which its output is too small to maintain the family, at whatever is considered to be the reasonable standard of living. The experts agree that under the average agro climatic conditions in India a farm well above two hectares will be capable of reconciling the various minimal of income and employment. The solution of the problem may partly be found in the agricultural land ceiling. The basic idea of the agricultural land ceiling is to ration out land in such a way that above a certain maximum limit, the land is taken away from the present holders and is distributed to landless or small holders according to some priorities. The objectives of ceiling strategy are to increase agricultural productivity of arable lands with a much more equitable income and power distribution and with a new structure suited for technological changes.

Since independence, in India, a number of steps have been taken to make structural changes in the agrarian societies and land reforms. The Kumarappa Committee, also known as the Congress Committee of Agrarian Reforms, recommended comprehensive measures for land distribution, creation of basic holdings, tenancy reforms, organization of small cooperative reforms and minimum agricultural wages. But so powerful was the lobby of the big and middle class peasants that the recommendations were shelved. The enthusiasm for land ceiling is much greater now, but it is doubtful whether the results will be encouraging. As a matter of fact, land reform is costly and has profound social consequences, but what is socially just may not be economically efficient or politically tenable.

4. Labour:

The availability of labour is also a major constraint in the agricultural land use and cropping patterns of a region. Labour represents all human services other than decision making and capital. The availability of labour, its quantity and quality at the periods of peak labour demand have great influence on decision making process of the farmer. The different crops and agrarian systems vary in their total labour requirements. The labour inputs vary considerably round the year for most of the agricultural enterprises with the result that many farmers employ a mixed system of production in order to keep their labour fully employed. Even then, in many parts of India, seasonal unemployment remains on most of the holdings, while during the peak periods of crop sowing (rice, wheat, sugarcane, vegetables and potatoes) and harvesting, there occurs acute shortage of labour which influences the sowing and harvesting operations and thereby affect the decision of a farmer whether to grow or not a crop.

Many of the cultivators of western Uttar Pradesh (Saharanpur and Muzaffarnagar districts) have given up the cultivation of rice owing to the non-avail- ability of workers at the times of transplantation and harvesting. The farmers of Punjab are increasingly dependent on Bihari labourers for the harvest of their wheat and rice crops. In many of the developed countries like the United States, Germany, Japan and U K, and in some tracts of the developing countries like the plains of the Punjab and Haryana in India, the rapid loss of farm labour is becoming a matter of great concern.

There are two basic reasons for the decline of agricultural labour, especially in the developed countries, such as US. Firstly, the industrialized nations offer alternative and financially attractive employment. Secondly, there are greater leisure opportunities for the industrial workers. In India, China developing countries, very few job opportunities occur outside agriculture which lead to unemployment of agricultural landless labour and small size farmers. Thus, the availability of labour has a direct impact in the labour intensive cropping patterns and its importance is much felt in the plantation estates and the subsistence paddy farming typology.

5. Redicing Capital And Artificial intelligent Mechanization and Equipment need:

Capital subscribes definite limitations to the selection of crops. Agricultural inputs like the livestock, irrigation, seeds, fertilizers, insecticides, pesticides, feeding stuffs, labour, purchase of land, machinery, carts, vehicles, various agricultural equipment's, buildings, fuel and power, sprays, veterinary services and repairs and maintenance require capital. All the farmers make their decisions on the basis of capital to invest.

The traditional way of cultivation is giving way to the market oriented crops which need more capital for getting higher returns. In the underdeveloped countries, moneylender is still the main source of finance in the remote rural areas and he advances money to the farmers at a high rate of interest with the intention of exploitation. Moreover, the permanent investment in agricultural system like plantation (tea, coffee, rubber) put a great restriction on the selection of alternative cropping patterns.

The development of irrigation facilities without capital is not possible. The role of irrigation in the areas of erratic rainfall, arid and semiarid regions is quite significant. Its importance has substantially increased after the adoption of High Yielding Varieties(HYV) in the developing countries. Irrigation not only enhances the yields of crops, it also helps in the intensification and horizontal expansion of agriculture. The development of irrigation which is one of the primary bases of agriculture needs enormous amount of capital. So, new agricultural machines, such as robotic will increase needs to any countries farmers.

The technological changes including the use of modern hand tools, animals drawn implements, tractors, thrashers and more economic patterns of farm management play a vital role in the selection of crops grown and decision making at the farm level. These changes help in improving the crop yields.

The improvements occur partly from the use of more effective equipment but also, because mechanization makes it possible to carry out farming operations more quickly and at the precise time calculated to maximize outputs. In the plains of the Punjab and western Uttar Pradesh, for example, the increasing substitution of tractors for bullocks has greatly shortened the time; the farmer has to spent on the ploughing and sowing of the kharif and rabi crops. This enables the farmers to cultivate their fallow land before it becomes infested with weeds in the summer season—a practice which was not feasible when oxen drawn plough was used. The result was a substantial diminution of weeds and increased cereal crop yields. More far-reaching is the impact of rice planting, and harvesting machines in Japan and China, where traditional methods entail the putting in of every single seedling of rice by hand at an immense cost and back-breaking toil.

In China, simple machines, constructed mostly of bamboo, wood and a few metal parts, have been in use since 1958. The machines, under normal conditions, do twenty times the amount of work of a hand planter, thus greatly shortening the time needed to plant the rice crop. The deployment of such machines is especially important for areas with two or more than two crops a year. The improved tools and farm implements can change appreciably the cropping patterns, cropping intensity and crop combinations resulting into high agricultural returns. In fact, tractors have largely transformed the agricultural landscape of the Punjab and Haryana in India.

6. Transportation Facilities:

Transportation facilities also have a direct bearing on the cropping patterns of a region. Better transport linkages are advantageous because of the economies in farm labour and storage costs which they make possible. These savings in turn help to make it economic for farmers to buy fertilizers and better equipment's. Better transport also makes it possible for farmers to put their less accessible land to more productive use.

In areas inadequately served by the modern means of

transportation, the surplus produce is often damaged either by adverse weather or by rats, pests and diseases. In the hilly states of northeast India (Meghalaya, Mizoram, Nagaland, Manipur, Arunachal Pradesh) costly crops like ginger, pineapple and banana are grown in surplus quantities but the poor means of transportation and inadequate road linkages deprive the cultivators of most of the profits. Contrary to this, in the United States, the truck farming is done at distant places from the big cities and markets as the farmer is able to supply his perishable crops (vegetables, flowers and fruits) to the distant markets within a short period of time at a reasonable rate of transportation.

7. Marketing Facilities:

The accessibility to the market is a major consideration in the decision making of the farmer. The intensity of agriculture and the production of crops decline as the location of cultivation gets away from the marketing centres. This is particularly noticeable when a bulky but low value crop has to be transported to the market. If it takes much time to send the produce, especially at the peak time, to the market when the farmer could have been profitably employed in other activities. The marketing system also influences the decision making of the farmer. In most of the countries the agricultural commodity markets are controlled by the buyers rather than sellers.

The farmers, however, can influence the market by storing their products on the farms or in cold storages until prices are remunerative. But since the number of buyers is lesser than the number of sellers and the cultivator is not financially well off to store the crop, the bargaining position of the farmer remains weak. The fluctuations in prices of agricultural produce many a times compel the farmers to change the cropping patterns.

Thus, the size of market may be an important factor because a market may encourage transport and handling innovations together with economic scale. Wheat has a great international market because it is convenient to handle even though it is a bulky commodity. Great Britain which imports about 8 million tonnes (metric tonnes) of wheat and other cereals has encouraged the development of special carrying ships, the opening of new water routes, such as the Hudson Bay from the Canadian wheat lands and the construction of new railway systems in the country.

8. Government Policies:

The agricultural land use and cropping patterns are also influenced by the government policies. The fluctuations in the price of sugarcane, wheat, oilseeds and legumes provide impetus or disincentives to the cultivators to grow these crops. Under certain political conditions, the government may stop the farmers to grow certain crops.

In the socialist countries like Russia, Romania, Bulgaria, Albania, Cuba, etc., the combination of crops, their rotation, a real strength and mode of disposal are completely controlled by the governments. In developing countries, like India, the government announces the price of various cereals and cash crops well in advance so that the farmers may devote their agricultural lands to different suitable cereal and other money fetching crops.

Apart from the domestic policies, the governments enter into international agreements to supply certain agricultural commodities to each other in order to maintain the balance of trade. The British government imports a substantial quantity of dairy products from New Zealand and Australia. Canada and Argentina export wheat while Cuba, Indonesia and India are the exporters of sugar. These international agreements have a close bearing on the cropping patterns of different countries.

9. Religion:

The religion of the cultivators has also influenced the agricultural activities in the different parts of the world. Each of the major religions has certain taboos and the use of certain agricultural commodities is prohibited in each of them. The Khasis and Lushais of Meghalaya and Mizoram are not interested in dairying as milk and milk products are taboo in their society. Piggery is prohibited among the Muslims, Hindus hate slaughtering, while Sikhs never go for the cultivation of tobacco.

The productive and adequately irrigated loamy tracts of western Haryana (including Bhiwani, Hissar, Mohindergarh, and Sirsa districts) are ideally suited for the cultivation of sunflower. It is a short duration highly remunerative cash crop which matures in only 60 days. For the last two decades, the farmers in these districts were obtaining two sunflower crops in a year in between the kharif and rabi crops. Unfortunately, the population of Neelgai (an antelope) has multiplied in this region significantly. This antelope which is being considered as sacred cow relishes the plant of sunflower and prefers to stay in or around its fields. The Neelgai menace has forced the cultivators of Haryana to give up sunflower cultivation. It is one of the unique examples in which the wild animals have influenced the cropping pattern significantly and the progressive farmers of Haryana are being deprived of a highly remunerative cash crop. Keeping into mind the religious sentiments of the Hindu farmers and the importance of sunflower as a cash crop (oilseed), the government should evolve a suitable strategy to check the fast growth of Neelgai population, failure to which the process of agricultural development in the region may be adversely affected.

In brief, the socioeconomic and politico cultural factors, especially land tenancy, landownership, size of holdings, fragmentation of fields, availability of labour, capital, accessibility to the market, storage facilities, government policies, international agreements and religion of the cultivators substantially influence the agricultural patterns and agricultural land use of a region.

How tea farming industry influences developing countries growth

● Which aspects will influence GDP growth

Agriculture accounts for 46.3 percent of the nation's Gross domestic Product (GDP), 83.9 percent of exports, and 80% of the labour force.The biggest countries in agriculture are leaders in production of wheat, rice, pulses etc. The top agricultural nations are China. India, USA. Indonesia etc.o research why and how farming development can influence GDP growth. China has the largest GDP in the world. It produced $25.3 trillion in 2018. But its GDP per capita was only $18,120 because it has four times the number of people as the United States. So, to research how agricultural development can bring GDP growth rapidly . We need research on these several aspects how US apply technology to innovate farming productivities skills:

On Agricultural Baseline aspect

USDA (United States Department of Agriculture Economic Research Service) Agricultural Projections report provides longrun projections for the farm sector for the next 10 years. These annual projections cover agricultural commodities, agricultural trade, and aggregate indicators of the sector, such as farm income. USDA's long-term agricultural projections provide a scenario for the farm sector for the next 10 years. Projections cover agricultural commodities, agricultural trade, and aggregate indicators of the sector such as farm income. The projections identify major forces and uncertainties affecting future agricultural markets; prospects for global long-term economic growth, consumption, and trade; and future price trends, trade flows, and U.S. exports of major farm commodities.

ERS economists participate in the long-term projections analysis and lead the preparation of the USDA long-term projections report. Other USDA offices and agencies involved in the long-term agricultural projections process include the World Agricultural Outlook Board, the Farm Programs and Conservation Business Center, the Foreign Agricultural Service, the Office of the Chief Economist, the Office of Budget and Program Analysis, the Risk Management Agency, the Agricultural Marketing Service, the Natural Resources Conservation Service, and the National Institute of Food and Agriculture.

James Hansen and Erik Dohlman (2020) reported that ERS provides three annual outputs covering agricultural baseline projections as below:

The Agricultural Baseline Projections Report, released in February each year, provides projections for the farm sector for the next 10 years. See the most recent report USDA Agricultural Projections to 2029.

The Agricultural Baseline Database provides 10-year projections from USDA's annual long-term projections report, which is published in February each year. The database covers projections for major field crops (corn, sorghum, barley, oats, wheat, rice, soybeans, and upland cotton) and livestock (beef, pork, poultry and eggs, and dairy), starting with the February 2000 report.

International Baseline Projections data indicate supply,

demand, and trade for major agricultural commodities for selected countries. These projections provide foreign country detail supporting the annual USDA agricultural baseline, which provides longrun, 10-year projections.

So, in long term, US will develop high technological agricultural industry to different projects. It will influence US GDP growth in rapid speed in the future.

Reference

James Hansen and Erik Dohlman, Agricultural Baseline Projections. Source: https://www.ers.usda.gov/topics/farm-economy/agricultural-baseline, February 18, 2020

On Agricultural Research and Productivity Aspect

Advances in agricultural productivity have led to abundant and affordable food and fiber throughout most of the developed world. Public and private agricultural research has been the foundation and basis for much of this growth and development. ERS data, research, and analyses quantify agricultural productivity improvements and the sources of improvement, in the U.S. and globally. A major focus is on developing indices of productivity growth that accurately reflect changes in the quality and mix of both inputs and outputs in the agricultural production process.

Keith Fuglie el. (Jan 2020) reported that ERS-compiled statistics (see the ERS data product, Agricultural Research Funding in the Public and Private Sectors) show that since about 1980, growth rates in public R&D in the United States have been generally slow. Levels of private investment have generally been higher, but with greater variation. In the early 2000s, public and private agricultural research investments began to diverge more rapidly. Real (inflation-adjusted) spending for private agricultural and food R&D nearly doubled between 2003 and 2013, while real public R&D spending fell. By 2010, private R&D for agricultural inputs alone surpassed the public level for all research.

ERS research finds that growth rates in public R&D in high-income countries as a group have also slowed, see Agricultural Research Investment and Policy Reform in High-Income Countries (ERR-249, May 2018). For high-income countries as a group, public agricultural research expenditures (adjusted for inflation) grew rapidly after 1960. However, growth slowed markedly in recent decades and has now turned negative. In constant 2011 dollars, public agricultural R&D spending in these countries grew from $3.9 billion in 1960 to a peak of $18.6 billion in 2009, before declining to $17.5 billion by 2013 (the latest year with complete data). This decline in public R&D spending marked the first sustained fall in agricultural R&D investment by these countries in 50 years, and was most pronounced in the United States and Southern Europe. The United States continues to lead among high-income countries in public agricultural R&D spending, but the U.S. share of the total declined from 35 percent in 1960 to less than 25 percent by 2013. See also the May 2018 Amber Waves article, Agricultural Research in High-Income Countries Faces New Challenges as Public Funding Stalls. Also see the ERS data product, International Agricultural Productivity.

To estimate the likely impacts of public research and development (R&D) funding choices on productivity growth, ERS projected future productivity growth with alternative public R&D investment scenarios. This analysis found that declines in public R&D have a more pronounced effects in the longrun than in the short-term. Even if public R&D investment recovers, future productivity growth (in terms of total factor productivity) would take some time to resume due to the lag between research investment and application. See the September 2015 Amber Waves feature, U.S. Agricultural Productivity Growth: The Past, Challenges, and the Future for more information.

Models and data decompose the sources of growth in global agricultural output. Globally, productivity growth accounts for a rising share of the increase in agricultural production, easing pressure on natural resources to supply the rising demand for food and agricultural commodities (see the ERS data product, International Agricultural Productivity, Growth in Global Agricultural Productivity: An Update (Amber Waves magazine, November 2013), and Accelerating Productivity Growth Offsets Decline in Resource Expansion in Global Agriculture (Amber Waves, September 2010).

Thus, On Agricultural Research and Productivity Aspect, US such as one developed country , it will achieve different kinds of agricultural technological innovation methods or techniques in order to raise itelf country's agricultural productivities number rapidly. Then, US GDP growth speed will be possible to increase rapidly .

Reference

Keith Fuglie, Sun Ling Wang, and Eric Njuki , Agricultural Research and Productivity .https://www.ers.usda.gov/ topics/farm-economy/agricultural-research-and-productivity,January 13, 2020

Productivity Is the Major Driver of U.S. Farm Sector's Economic Growth. According to the latest statistics, Paul Heisey and Keith Fuglie (2018) they indicated , the level of U.S. farm output nearly tripled between 1948 and 2017, growing at an average annual rate of 1.53 percent. USDA's Economic Research Service (ERS) researchers attribute this growth mainly to productivity advancement.

To monitor the performance of the U.S. farm sector, ERS develops productivity statistics along with price and quantity estimates of 10 output sub-categories (such as meat animals, dairy, and food grains) and 12 input sub-categories (such as hired labor, durable equipment, and pesticides). ERS's agricultural productivity statistics are based on a broad productivity measure that reflects all inputs, called total factor productivity (TFP). Annual TFP growth is the difference between the growth of aggregate agricultural output and the growth of aggregate inputs used on farms under the control of farmers.

Reference
Paul Heisey and Keith Fuglie, Agricultural Research Investment and Policy Reform in High- Income Countries , https://www.ers.usda.gov/amber-waves/2020/july/productivity-is-the-major-driver-of-us-farm-sector-s-economic-growthby , ERS, May 2018

● How does the tea agriculture sector affect the Malawi economy?

Tea is the most popular drink in the world after water – an estimated 70,000 cups are drunk every second. Yet tea farmers and workers struggle to get a fair deal. This can have a very real and human cost. One in four children in Kenya's tea and coffee-growing regions are malnourished, leading to stunted growth. One in 10 children in the tea-growing regions of Malawi die before their fifth birthday.Tea is produced on large plantations or estates and picked by employed workers. It is also grown on small plots of land by smallholder farmers who sell their freshly-plucked green leaf to plantations or tea factories for processing into black tea.

In Africa, the average smallholder's farm is less than half

the size of a football pitch. Tea farmers face the challenge of low and fluctuating prices for the green leaf they sell, and a lack of power in a tea supply chain dominated by large companies. On tea estates, the challenges for workers vary depending on the origin. Workers may face low wages, long working hours and a difficult relationship with estate management. Often it is the management they depend on for basic needs such as housing, healthcare, access to water and even education for their children.

Kenya's agricultural sector directly influences overall economic performance through its contribution to GDP. Periods of high economic growth rates have been synonymous with increased agricultural growth. The tea sector is a dominant sector and the coffee sector has started to pick up following a decline in the recent past. Malawi is one owning the natural environment to grow tea country. In 2019, Malawi's economic growth is projected to reach 4.4%, increasing over the medium term to 5.0 - 5.5%. Growth in 2019 is buoyed by a good harvest overall, despite the impact Cyclone Idai. Solid agricultural growth is likely to support agro-processing and households' disposable incomes, which should, in turn, drive the service sector.

Malawai

Population live in rural areas. Tea is one of the country's most important industries and main export crops. Tea is Malawi's biggest employer, with 50,000 people working in the sector. While these jobs pay above the national average, tea workers remain poor. The 16,500 small-scale tea farmers in Malawi also find it challenging to make a decent income and provide for their families. Poor diets are a fundamental issue in Malawi, and malnutrition is one of the reasons why one in ten children in tea-growing regions don't live past the age of five.

However, Malawi is highly vulnerable to climate change, which affects where and how tea can be grown. The impact of deforestation in the country has been significant, causing flash floods and limiting firewood for the rural population. Both small farmer organisations owned and governed by the farmers themselves and tea plantations that comply with strict Fairtrade Standards for hired labour can become Fairtrade certified. Fairtrade Standards for tea include an origin-specific Fairtrade Minimum Price, which acts as a safety net against the unpredictable market. Standards also include payment of the additional Fairtrade Premium of US$ 0.50/kg black tea, for producers to invest as they see fit. Examples include putting resources into better farming so they can earn more money for their crops, or it could be for education, clean water and clinics for the community. 392,700 farmers and workers across 11 countries are involved in Fairtrade tea production. 10,700 tonnes of tea was sold as Fairtrade in 2017. This means certified farmers and workers earned €5.3 million in Fairtrade Premium in 2017. On plantations, workers invest almost half of their Premium in community services such as housing, education and healthcare. However, Fairtrade certified organisations sell only around 7 percent of their tea on Fairtrade terms – this means they don't benefit from being certified to the extent that they could. So, natural good environment can help Malawi to grow any kinds of tea in order to raise different kinds of tea taste to supply to export to different countries tea markets in order to satisfy tea drinkers' drinking need seriously. So, tea industry will be Malawi's main agricultural income source ,even it can compete to any other tea export competitors and it can also create many tea growing and tea manufacture job chances to many tea workers in Malawi. Consequently, Malawai's tea export will help it to raise GDP growth rapidly.

Economists opinions to old and new economic social development

Our societies are experiencing new economic social development stage from old economic social development stage. What are the economists' opiunions or view points concern how and why our societies are experiencing new econoomic social change. What can influence to our social changes from new economic development. I shall attempt to apply some economic theories to explain why some economic theories are not be accepted to our nowadays new economic social development as below:

Firstly, the invisible hand theory changes, it is not be accepted to our nowadays new economic socical development need absolutely. It indicates that the wealth of nations marshels the theories of self interest first written about in the theory of moral sentiments into a way of looking at how societies prosper. Smith believed that real wealth was the sum of the annual produce of the land and labour of the whole country and that prosperity was based on increasing that.

He focused on the concept of natural liberty , the idea that people can deploy their resources in competition with others. This process would identify which activities were most worth doing. For example, if mining produced higher returns than the average of other activities than capital would naturally swing towards that area and away from less productive areas. It is are good example for old economic invisible hand theory.

However, our societies are changing. Smith's opinions toward the mining industry that produces the greatest value, so each worker aims for the job that will make him or her the most money.

In this case, as Smith put it, this worker " neither intends to promote the public interest, not knows how much hs is promoting it". He intends only his own gain, and he is in this led by an invisible hand to promote and which was no part of his intention. But, nowadays societies, any labours will needs to intend to help their organizations to promote the public interest, he or she needs to know how much she/she is promoting it. For this mining company example, the mining worker needs to know whether their mining tasks value is how much, when they are seeking the mining land can have how much market value for their organizations. It can gain how much profit. Because if their mining company can have high mining land value to help them to produce the good quality of mines products to sell, then they can help themselves organizations to earn high profit indirectly. Consequently, these mining worker individual wage may also be also influenced to raise.Hence, these mining workers' value is depended on whether their mining tasks can bring how much mining land value to let their mining company to sell in order to earn high or less mining

sale income in this global competitive mining market.

Hence, new economy theory explained that the invisible hand means that any labor will also need to concern or intent to promote the public interest for themselves employers, instead of doing the job to earn income, becacause when they can help their employers to promote the public interest to achieve higher social value interest to themselve organizations, then their employers can earn more profit when sale growth is influenced to raise by promoting the higher public interest. Consequently, nowadays our societies, any company's labours' wages may also be influenced to raised by their promoting interest (invisible hand method).

Secondly, the division of labour concept that is explained by Smith, he indicated the greatest improvement in the productive process of labour.... seem(s) to have been the effects of the effects of the division of labour, Smith wrote. However, it has been changing to an office or a factory , its working enviroment was seen to have difference to the division of labur view. Smith was writing the birth stage of the industrial revolution that over time would see hundreds of thousands of people drawn into mass production factories in old economic society.

BUt, nowadays our societies' manufacturing technology is improved, such as manufacturing robotic technology can assist a team of workers to cooperate to work in order to achieve high efficient productivities.Smith could see how better organized work lead to greater output by each worker, called " productivity". It is significant that his theory was based on the observation of actual economic activity rather than on irorytower supposition. He realised that one untrained worker left to his factory that makes pins, drawing out the wire, straighting it, cutting it, pointing it, grinding it. Smoith estimated that ten workers could produce 48,000 a day or 4,800 each. How to achieve a 4,800 per cent increase in productivity, he indicated three factors as below:

These three factors include:

(1) Each worker becomes more skilled in his/her particular contribution ever time,

(2) Time is saved by workers not having to swap machines

and equipment as they go through each
individual task as well as
(3) This encourages the design of machines that make is easier to do the work.

But, nowadays, pin factory may apply pin robotic machines to help them to increase pins productivities in short time. It implies that future division of labours or organized labours method won't be important to help pins productivities number increases. When robotic machines can replace any different pins departments part tasks efficiently, even their productive pins performance can be better than any one of the factory's different departments oin workers' tasks more easily.

Hence, in new economic society, some manufacturing industry's dividion of labour concept can not be adapted , due to robotic manufacturing machines invention. It can replace any organizations' workers tasks of manufacturing lines in any one manufacturing organizaton's team more easily and efficiently. However, in the old economic society, division of labour explains why workers on a car production line eash add some part to the basic chassis, but in the new economic society, car robots can replace different car manufacturing part tasks worker to do their different tasks on a car production line or why busy bankers do not answer the phone themselves because speaking robots may help buysy bankers to answer the phone or supermarkets do not need warwhouse workers to help them to deliver goods in warehouses, because warehouse robots can replace them to deliver goods in warehouses rapidly.

So, in new economic society, division of labour concept can not be accepted to some kinds of manufacturing industries, even service industries, due to robots can replace any workers or service staffs to do their tasks efficiently. In our nowadays society, because technology innovation, such as robotic manufacturing machine invention, it may help any organizations need many workers to worker in any manufacturing line or team. So, division of labour concept won't be adopted to any one nowadays factories or offices environment when robots can be participated to the office or factory or warehouse's working environment.

Surplus value of labour theory is Marx's economic theory. He too looks at commodities and the way the things are produced. He saw value arising from the effort, that the workers put in to produce the goods. So, the amount of labour used to make goods determined their prices over sell for the long run. Mars focused on value. In this view, the amount of labour determined the value of goods produced. For example, a machine takes five hours to make something has twice the value as make something has hours. He distinguished between use value and the exchange value that the owners of the goods could get by selling it. Marx gave opinions to indicate that a machine worker would be paid a wage to produce a box-worth of tools that would sell for a much higher price than this daily wage.

Think of supermarket checkout worker, a solicitor's assistant or a bank teller, these staffs may be paied higher salaries to compare factory manufacturing workers , office cleaners , because they can help their employers to bring more clients , when they can serve their clients or factory workers do not need to serve clients. So, they are different to think or judge whether their performances are excellent ot worse in order to making rising wage decision more easily.

However, it is old economic social view point to determine the surplus value of labour aspect. Inold economic view point, Marx saw that there wa a difference between what the workers were paid for their efforts and what the factory owners received as a result. Marx called this " surplus value": Th capitalists were able to keep the exta value of profits because they owned the means of production.

Capitalists therefore need to pay the workers less than the value at which they planned to sell the goods. This equation also needs to include the costs of the machinery, which Marx explains as being the value of the " concealed labour" that next in to build the machine. Their profit was the surplus divided by the sum of the labour costs (variable capitals) and machines (fixed capital).

Marx also saw that the factory owner would look the pay the minimum that the workers needed for them and their families to survive, call " subsistence wage". He said that this wage was kept to low by the existence of unemployed people ready to seek now work in society. Thus, Marx felt factory workers ar paid less wage, but service workers are paid high wage because service workers can help employers to serve clients to let they feel satisfactory service. Then clients number will be influenced to increase by whom excellent service. So, the excellent performance service staffs can increase higher salaries to compare general non-service workers.

However, in our new economic societies, surplus value of labour concept can not be accepted, because our nowadays societies, this pool was kept filled by technological , such as robots can do service tasks, e.g. shopping center front line client service tasks, security tasks, even restaurant cooking tasks, instead of warehouse, factory, manufacturing tasks. So, technological advances that reduced the need for labour to future service and manufacturing industries. This is one new service or manufacturing technological opinions or ideas to service or manufacturing labour is kust another commodity only that can be bought and sold, with its value being equal to the cost of kept is for work.

Hence, when servicing or manufacturing robots are popular ro be used to any factories, offices, restaurants, shopping centers , warehouses etc. workplaces. The service workers and manufacturing workers their wages or wages won't be have much difference, because robots may replace to do their tasks to serve their clients or manufacture any kinds of products in any organizations in any time.

It seems that service workers' wages won't be increased more easily to compare non-service workers' salaries. They may be seemed to such a commodity. When the organization decides to apply robots to replace some service or manufaturing workers to do their tasks in their teams. Hence, the surplus value of labour theory won't be accepted to the organizations when they choose robots to replace some or the department's all manufacturing workers or service workers to do their tasks.

The organization's surplus value of labour is depended whether it decides to apply robots to help it to manufacture any kinds of products or serve to their clients in nowadays new economic society.

How applying economy theories solve economic problems

The economic problem – sometimes called the basic or central economic problem – asserts that an economy's finite resources are insufficient to satisfy all human wants and needs. Economics involves the study of how to allocate resources in conditions of scarcity However, viewing economics as the study of how society allocates resources can lead to conflation of normative economic planning and empirical study of how economic agents operate in these conditions.

In mainstream neoclassical economics, it is assumed that humans pursue their self-interest, and that the market mechanism best satisfies the various wants different individuals might have. These wants are often divided into individual wants (which depend on the individual's preferences and purchasing power parity) and collective wants (which are the wants of entire groups of people). Things such as food and clothing can be classified as either wants or needs, depending on what type and how often a good is requested.

However, economists have sometimes characterized "how" to produce as a "technological problem" of efficiency whereas the allocation of what is produced is an "economic problem". In a free market, the "how" of production and allocation of resources is distributed among economic agents. In a centrally planned economy, a principal decides how and what to produce on behalf of agents. Modern economies are often welfare capitalist with various regulations, which makes the economic system more equitable while retaining the distributed free market system. Due to human wants are unlimited, an infinite series of human wants remains continue with human life.Nobody can claim that all of his wants have been satisfied and he has no need to satisfy any further want. Everybody feels hunger at a time then other he needs water. Sometime one feels the desire of clothing then starts to feel the desire of having good conveyance. When all existing wants are satisfied then new wants starts to create in mind, so the series of wants remains continue till the last moment of life. So an economic problem arises because of existence of unlimited human wants.

Problem of allocation of resources

The problem of allocation of resources arises due to the scarcity of resources, and refers to the question of which wants should be satisfied and which should be left unsatisfied. In other words, what to produce and how much to produce. More production of a good implies more resources required for the production of that good, and resources are scarce. These two facts together mean that, if a society decides to increase production of some good, it has to withdraw some resources from the production of other goods. In other words, more production of a desired commodity can be made possible only by reducing the quantity of resources used in the production of other goods.

The problem of allocation deals with the question of whether to produce capital goods or consumer goods. If the community decides to produce capital goods, resources must be withdrawn from the production of consumer goods. In the long run, however, [investment] in capital goods augments the production of consumer goods. Thus, both capital and consumer goods are important. The problem is determining the optimal production ratio between the two.

In fact, in our societies, resources are scarce and it is important to use them as efficiently as possible. Thus, it is essential to know if the production and distribution of national product made by an economy is maximally efficient. The production becomes efficient only if the productive resources are utilized in such a way that any reallocation does not produce more of one good without reducing the output of any other good. In other words, efficient distribution means that redistributing goods cannot make anyone better off without making someone else worse off. (See Pareto efficiency.) So, scientists will apply efficient distribution methods to help any countries to earn the absolute advantages when we buy and sell any kinds of products or food between ourselves countries, e.g. when US has good natural resource to grow any food, e.g. potato, wheat , vegatable, cotton , then US can export to sell to China, because China has no any farms to grow agriculture food to supply itself Chinese to eat. So, China must need to buy any agriculture food from US. Otherwise, China has cheap labor to supply to US any manufacturers to help them to manufacture their electronic products. SO, it has many US factories are built in China to let Chinese workers help them to produce their products because their wages are cheaper to compare US workers. So, comparative economic advantage will be choice to apply between US and China both countries. (Absolute advantge trade theory).

The inefficiencies of production and distribution exist in all types of economies. The welfare of the people can be increased if these inefficiencies are ruled out. Some cost must be incurred to remove these inefficiencies. If the cost of removing these inefficiencies of production and distribution is more than the gain, then it is not worthwhile to remove them.

The problem of full employment of resources
(the division of labour concept and Surplus value of labour theory)

In view of how to use available resources are fully utilized is an important one. A community should achieve maximum satisfaction by using the scarce resources in the best possible manner—not wasting resources or using them inefficiently. There are two types of employment of resources:

(1) Labour-intensive

(2) Capital-intensive

In capitalist economies, however, available resources are not fully used. In times of depression, many people want to work but can't find employment. It supposes that the scarce resources are not fully utilized in a capitalistic economy.

The problem of economic growth

If productive capacity grows, an economy can produce progressively more goods, which raises the standard of living. The increase in productive capacity of an economy is called economic growth. There are various factors affecting economic growth. The problems of economic growth have been discussed by numerous growth models, including the Harrod-Domar model, the neoclassical growth models of Solow and Swan, and the Cambridge growth models of Kaldor and Joan Robinson. This part of the economic problem is studied in the economies of development.

Needs and wants problems

Needs are things or material items of peoples need for survival, such as food, clothing, housing, and water. Everyone has a different needs and wants. Until the Industrial Revolution, the vast majority of the world's population struggled for access to basic human needs.

Wants are effective desires for a particular product, or for something that can only be obtained by working for it. While the fundamental needs of survival are key in the function of the economy, wants are the driving force that stimulates demand for goods and services. To curb the economic problem, economists must classify the nature and different wants of consumers, as well as prioritize wants and organize production to satisfy as many wants as possible.

Five bases problems of economy

In our societies , in general, our societies will have these similar problems The following points highlight the five basic problems of an economy. The problems are: 1. What to Produce and in What Quantities? 2. How to Produce these Goods? 3. For whom is the Goods Produced? 4. How Efficiently are the Resources being Utilised? 5. Is the Economy Growing?.

Problem 1:What to Produce and in What Quantities?

The first central problem of an economy is to decide what goods and services are to be produced and in what quantities. This involves allocation of scarce resources in relation to the composition of total output in the economy. Since resources are scarce, the society has to decide about the goods to be produced: wheat, cloth, roads, television, power, buildings, and so on. Once the nature of goods to be produced is decided, then their quantities are to be decided. How many tonnes of wheat, how many televisions, how many million kws of power, how many buildings, etc. Since the resources of the economy are scarce, the problem of the nature of goods and their quantities has to be decided on the basis of priorities or preferences of the society.

If the society gives priority to the production of more consumer goods now, it will have less in the future. A higher priority on capital goods implies less consumer goods now and more in the future. But since resources are scarce, if some goods are produced in larger quantities, some other goods will have to be produced in smaller quantities. Suppose the economy produces capital goods and consumer goods. In deciding the total output of the economy, the society has to choose that combination of capital goods and consumer goods which is in keeping with its resources.

Problem 2: How to Produce these Goods?

The next basic problem of an economy is to decide about the techniques or methods to be used in order to produce the required goods. This problem is primarily dependent upon the availability of resources within the economy. If land is available in abundance, it may have extensive cultivation. If land is scarce, intensive methods of cultivation may be used. If labour is in abundance, it may use labour-intensive techniques; while in the case of labour shortage, capital-intensive techniques may be used.

The technique to be used also depends upon the type and quantity of goods to be produced. For producing capital goods and large outputs, complicated and expensive machines and techniques are required. On the other hand, simple consumer goods and small outputs require small and less expensive machines and comparatively simple techniques.

Further, it has to be decided what goods and services are to be produced in the public sector and what goods and services in the private sector. But in choosing between different methods of production, those methods should be adopted which bring about an efficient allocation of resources and increase the overall productivity in the economy.

Problem 3. For whom is the Goods Produced?

The third basic problem to be decided is the allocation of goods among the members of the society. The allocation of basic consumer goods or necessities and luxuries comforts and among the household takes place on the basis of among the distribution of national income. Whosoever possesses the means to buy the goods may have then. A rich person may have a large share of the luxuries goods, and a poor person may have more quantities of the basic consumer goods he needs.

Problem 4: How Efficiently are the Resources being Utilised?

This is one of the important basic problems of an economy because having made the three earlier decisions, the society has to see whether the resources it owns are being utilised fully or not. In case the resources of the economy are lying idle, it has to find out ways and means to utilise them fully.

Problem 5: Is the Economy Growing?

The last and the most important problem is to find out whether the economy is growing through time or is it stagnant. If the economy is stagnant at any point inside the production possibility curve, it has to be moved on to the production possibility curve PP whereby the economy now produces larger quantities of consumer goods and capital goods. Economic growth takes place through a higher rate of capital formation which con?sists of replacing existing capital goods with new and more productive ones by adopting more efficient production techniques or through innovations.

All of these economy problems will be our societies often causes to anyone feels need to solve problems in order to achieve our societies can have enough resources to satisfy our every day living.

● rational consumer theory

The Consumer Problem

It seems that economic problems and consumer problems are similar, I feel that it is possible , economists can attempt to apply any economic theories to solve some consumer problems in some suitations. They can find the accurate solutions when they can apply the suitable economic theories to solve the suitable consumer or economic problems in our societies. I shall indicate that how economists can apply the suitable economic theories to attempt to solve some consumer problems in our societies as below:

Consumer theory is concerned with how a rational consumer would make consumption decisions. What makes this problem worthy of separate study, apart from the general problem of choice theory, is its particular structure that allows us to derive economically meaningful results. The structure arises because the consumer's choice sets sets are assumed to be de?ned by certain prices and the consumer's income or wealth. The consumer's problem is to choose that is most preferred or, equivalently, that has the greatest utility.

The assumption of perfect information is built deeply into the formulation of this choice problem, just as it is in the underlying choice theory. Some alternative models treat the consumer as rational but uncertain about the products, for example how a particular food will taste or a how well a cleaning product will perform. Some goods may be experience goods which the consumer can best learn about by trying ("experiencing") the good. In that case, the consumer might want to buy some now and decide later whether to buy more. That situation would need a di?erent formulation. Similarly,if the agent thinks that high price goods are more likely to perform in a satisfactory way, that, too, would suggest quite a di?erent formulation. Agents are price-takers. The agent takes prices p as known, ?xed and exogenous. This assumption excludes things like searching for better prices or bargaining for a discount.

● Demand And Supply Elastic Theory Solves Consumer Problems

What is economy rule predict consumer behaviour? Why and How does economist can apply economy rule to predict consumer behaviours? I shall explain the reasons as below:

Why does economic principle be the best to predict consumer behaviour. It may include these two reasons: The first focuses on the substantive domain of study, in this interpretation , economics is a social science devoted to understanding how the economy works. The second definition focuses on methods: economics is a way of doing social science, using particular tools. In this interpretation the discipline is associated with formal modelling and statistical analysis rather than particular hypotheses or theories about the economy. Therefore, economic methods can be applied to many other areas besides the economy, everything from decisions within the family to questions about political institutions.

Demand and supply principle predict public transport tool passenger behaviour

Economists need to use the right economic ideas to predict consumer behaviour. So, Misuse the wrong economy ideas to predict consumer behaviours. It will do more wrong judgement to evaluate or predict why and how and when the country's consumer behaviours will change. It is every economist needs to consider issue. For example, the economy idea application of economic supply-demand principles to public transport. Different fares would give commuters with more-flexible hours the incentive to avoid peak travel times. They would allow passenger traffic to spread out over time, reducing the pressure on the public transport system when enabling even larger total passenger flow. IT aims to reduce traffic congestion, increased public-transport use, reduced car-bon emissions and cause air pollution and generated considerable revenue for the country's transport system. So, if the country can apply supply and demand economic principle to attempt to predict how many passengers number needs to catch transport tools to go to work or go to school or other activities. Then, it can predict how many bus, ferry, taxi, train, underground train, tram etc. different public transport tools to satisfy future public transport passengers' needs in society. So, this demand and supply principle is the comparative best rule to predict any kinds of public transport passengers' road needs, when they need to either go to school, go to office, go to leisure or shopping etc. different kinds of activities. So, applying the demand and supply principle to predict road and sea public transport passengers can help the country to reduce air pollution when they feel that they can find any public transport tools to catch any time conveniently , then it can encourage them to reduce car purchase desire. When many people choose to catch public transport tools, then it will reduce many cars number on the road. Then, air pollution will reduce as well as any public transport tools' income will also increase as well as traffic jam will also reduce. When the country can evaluate how many people choose to catch bus or taxi or ferry or train or underground train, or tram or train etc. different kinds of public transport tools, then the country can predict the more accurate public transport tools number to every kind of public transport tool to satisfy their journey needs. e.g. whether underground train or train or tram need to decrease or increase the frequent times or number to catch the volume of passenger in busy or non-busy time; or whether bus company has need to increase how much buses to catch the city location passengers when they are living in the city. Moreover, supply and demand principle can help any public transport tools to explain why their passengers number reduces in the year, it may due to fare charge is unreasonable, feeling uncomfortable to sit on the seat or air condition is poor in the transport tool environment, or there are no more seats because many there are much time is full passenger and no seat vacancy to provide to them to sit .

So, supply and demand principle can help any kinds of public transport tools to find whether which is (are) the factor(S) can influence the current or last year passengers number reduce. Then, they can concentrate on improving their weaknesses to raise their service quality . So, supply and demand principle can also help they to evaluate whether what their weakness are in order to improve to increase passengers number. They can do questionnaires to enquiry their passengers' response to evaluate whether which areas of services that they feel unsatisfactory. So, the different kinds of service satisfactory feeling to the passengers number data will be the main source to help the kind of public transport tool to analyse and conclude the results more accurate, then they can make the more accurate judgement to improve the of service. For example, the questionnaires indicate that the many passengers feel the bus fare is reasonable, but many passengers feel they can not find any seats to sit easily. So, it implies that the bus firm ought buy more buses or enlarges bus size and increases more seats in the enlarged buses. Then, it does not reduce its fare but it needs to find solutions to let passengers can find seats to sit in every bus more easily. But, if the questionnaires indicate that there are many passengers feel its fare is higher or unreasonable to compare other kinds of public transportation tools. Hence, it can avoid to spend more expenditure to increase bus number to the city, if the city has many passengers , they still choose bus to catch, but they feel its fare is too higher to compare other kinds of public transport tool. Then, it only needs to reduce its fare , it ought help it to increase passengers number. Hence, demand and supply principle is the most suitable economic method to evaluate any kinds of public transport system passenger needs in any country nowadays.

● Supply and demand and price elasticities principle predict oil energy user behaviour

The another case is that demand and supply principle can predict oil buyer behaviour to find whether what factors can cause the oil buyer individual need reduces. For example , a rise in production costs increases market prices and reduces quantities demanded and supplied. Or when, energy cost rise, utility bills increases and households fid extra ways of saving heating and electricity. But, others are nor. For example, whether a tax is imposed on the producers or consumer of a commodity, say oil has nothing to do with who ends up paying for it. The tax might be administered on oil companies, but it might be consumers who really pay for it through higher prices at the pump. Or the extra cost might be imposed on consumers in the form of a sale tax, but the oil companies might be forces to absorb it through lower prices. It all depends on the " price elasticities" of demand and supply. With the addition of extra assumption, this model also generates rather strong implications about how well markets work. In particular, a competitive market economy is efficient in the sense that it is impossible to improve one person's well-being without reducing somebody.

● Demand and supply principle can misuse to predict consumer behaviour when the two firms participate advertisement to promote their products in the same time

Why can demand and supply principle misuse to predict consumer behaviour when the two firms participate advertisement to promote their products in the same time ? I shall explain as below: Assume that two competing firms must decide whether to have a big advertising budget. Advertising would allow one firm to steal some of the other's customers. But when they both advertise, the effects on customer demand cancel out. The firms end up having spent money needlessly.
We might expect that neither firm would choose to spend much on advertising, but the model shows that this logic is off base. When the firms make their choices independently and they care only about their own profits, each one has an incentive to advertise, regardless of what the other firm does. When the other firm does not advertise, you can steal customers from it if you do advertise, when the other firm does advertise, you have to advertise to prevent loss of customers. So, these two firms end up in a bad equilibrium in which both have to waste resources. This market can not apply demand and supply principle to predict consumer

behaviours because they depends advertisement to promote their products. If these two firms advertise their products in the same time. Then , it is not possible that if one firm increases it price and it will cause its customer number loss, due to its advertise can help it to attract customers to consider its product from television or radio or newspapers or magazine promotion channels. So, I suppose that these two firms decide to increase their price, when they advertise their products to let customers to know in the same time. They will not lose their customers or reduce their customers easily. Because their customers can be persuaded to choose to buy their products to compare other similar products in preference. So, their increasing price will not influence their customers number lose easily. It explains that demand and supply principle is not right to this case, so demand and supply principle can misuse to help them to predict consumer behaviours when they advertise their products in the same time. Also, demand and supply principle is not suitable to them to predict consumer behaviours when they advertise their products in the same time. They will do wrong prediction to their consumers purchase desire when they advertise their products in the same time.

ON conclusion, using these demand and supply and price elasticity techniques, economists derive specific prediction for how consumers choose which products to buy, how households save, how firms invest, how workers search for jobs, as well as for how these actions depend on the particulars. They can help them to predict job and consumption behaviours more accurate, it depends on whether the situation is right, such as both competition firms participate to advertise their products in the same time case, it is not right to apply above economic principle to predict consumer behaviours. They will get wrong prediction when they apply this principle to predict consumer behaviours.

However, demand and supply principle can predict below any one of these cases. I shall indicate as below:

The problem of need-based scholarships: Most systems for providing college scholarships are based on some definition of financial needs, with scholarships generally being given only to those students who must need financial help in order to attend school.

Is need, rather than academic ability, the best basic on which to choose those students who are to be encouraged to attend college? Which way of choosing who gets aids is the more just? Which is the more efficient ? Is the overall educational level of society increased more by giving financial aid to bright students or to needy students? Presumably the aid offers more leverage to needy students, since they all need the money in order to attend college, whereas, many of the bright students would attend college in any case. But is a smaller number of bright students the more important addition?

So, the school can apply demand and supply principle to predict whether how many parents feel need financial assistance and evaluate how much financial amount is the right to borrow. It aims to calculate how many parents feel real financial need and how much to lend to them in order to let these students to get the most fair financial assistance.

Assuming the school wish to use need as a basis, how does the school determines " financial need"? Is need a function or parents' income? What, then , does the school about children of wealthy parents who are living independently of them and get no aid from parents? Should they be punished for their parents' wealth? But if they are given aid, won't all students, in order to get aid, claim to be independent of their parents?

Is need solely a matter of family income, or should not the school takes a family's financial obligations into account? Does not it make more sense to give aid to someone whose parents must put night more children through school than to someone from a family of five or one only with the same income? But in a possible parallel situations, should a family that carries mortgages on one or two large homes get preference simply because they do not have much money left to spend on college? Does doing this reward ? Is there a difference between the case of night children and the case of the large mortgage? How should parents who are not married , but are living together and supporting their children jointly be counted? Most parents are supporter to their children , although they are married in possible.

So, the school needs to gather all these data to evaluate how many parents are not married or married or living with their children together, how much salary they earn as well as every family has how much children as well as whether they have mortgage for their houses. So, these number will be the financial education assistance demanders, but it does not represent their real financial needs. It is possible that someone does not feel any financial need, although their children apply financial assistance to your school. Then , your school needs to evaluate whether how much financial assistance can lend to every real financial need student family. It can not exceed your final financial expenditure budget (supply) , when your financial expenditure is not enough. SO, demand and supply principle can be applied to research this school real family financial demand to lend to the real financial need families and evaluate whether the reasonable financial amount to lend to every child family to study in your school.

● Supply and demand principle explains Why has it relationship between immigration to US these two regions immigrant number and wage?

A fascinating and important example of supply and demand, full of complexities, is the role of immigration in determining wages. If you ask people , they are likely to tell you that immigration into California or Florida US, surely lowers the wages of people in those regions. It is just supply and demand analysis of immigration. According to this analysis, of these to these two regions in US. Immigration in to a region shifts the supply curve for labor to the right and pushes down wages. Why has it relationship between immigration to US these two regions immigrant number and wage? Careful economic studies cast doubt on this simple proposition, however, a recent survey of the evidence concludes:

The effect of immigration on the labor market outcomes of natives is small in US. There is no evidence of economically significant reductions in native employment. Most analysis, finds that a 10 percent increase in the fraction of immigrants in the population reduced native wages by a most 1%.

How can we explain the small impact of immigration on wages? The main mistake is to forget how mobile the American population is and that the impact of immigration on wages, we must examine the effect of new immigrants when the strength of the local economy and the number of native-born residents in a city are unchanged, that is , when these other things are held constant. Unless you exclude the effects other changing variables, you can not accurately predict the impact of immigration. The same principle holds in doing a supply0and demand analysis of any market. As much as possible, when you are examining the impact of a supply or demand shift, you must try to keep all other things constant.

Rationing by prices theory

By determining the equilibrium prices and quantities of all inputs and outputs, the market allocated or rations out the scare goods of the society among the possible uses. Who does the rationing? A planning board? Congress or the president? BO, the markplace, through the interaction of supply and demand, doe the rationing. This is rationing by the purse.

What foods are produces? This is answered by the signals of the market price. High oil prices stimulates oil production, whereas low food prices drive resources out of agriculture. Those who have the most dollars votes have the greatest influences on what goods are produced. All of these considers how demand and supply to the market.

For whom are goods produces? The power of the pursue indicates the distribution of income and consumption. Those with higher incomes end up with larger houses, more clothing, and linger vacations. When the most urgently felt needs get fulfilled through through the demand curve.

Even, the how question is decided by supply and demand. When corn prices are low, it is not profitable for farmers to use expensive tractors and irrigation systems, and only the best land is cultivated. When oil prices are high, oil companies drill in deep offshore waters and employ novel seismic techniques to find oil.

IN sum , any thing needs through demands, interact with costs of goods, as reflected in supplies in our economic world. Hence, demand and supply theory ought be the most accurate method to help any businesses or governments to predict their shareholders behaviours when they will change as well as how and how their behaviours change.

Chapter 5

New Economic Consumer Choice Theory Solves Consumer Problems

What is 'consumer choice theory'?

'Consumer choice theory' is a hypothesis about why people buy things. Put simply, it says that you choose to buy the things that give you the greatest satisfaction, while keeping within your budget. At the heart of this theory are three assumptions about human nature?

The first assumption is that when you shop, you choose to buy things based on calculated decisions about what will make you happiest. In economics language, this is known as utility maximisation (Economists really like to put quite simple concepts into long complicated terms.)

Secondly, the theory assumes that no matter how much you shop, you will never be completely satisfied. In other words, you will always be happier consuming a little bit more. This is known as the principle of non-satiation.

Thirdly, even though you always get more happiness from more consumption, the amount of pleasure you get from each good decreases with the more you consume. So if you eat two ice creams rather than one, you get more overall pleasure, but the second ice-cream won't be as satisfying as the first. This is known as decreasing marginal utility.

Consumer choice theory has influenced everything from government policy to corporate advertising to academia.But the theory has been criticized for not being the most accurate description of how people actually make choices. A whole new branch of economics, called 'behavioral economics', has emerged essentially to use findings from psychology to disprove the assumptions behind consumer choice theory. This has also led others to argue that consumer choice theory is less about describing how we do actually behave, and is more about describing how people should behave.? In other words, by portraying people as self-interested shopaholics, economists are saying that is it okay and natural for us to be avid consumers.

Consumer choice theory can be applied to solve consumer problems during the country can have economic growth , the reasons may include as below:

The scenario leading to inflation starts with poor growth. Forget about everything that comes next and focus on that most important factor. Because it happens that the scenario leading to a budget crisis also starts with poor growth, and the scenario leading to a long-term unemployment crisis starts with poor growth, and a scenario leading to a begger-thy-neighbour trade crisis starts with poor growth, and so on. So a very important question is: what can be done to improve the prospects for economic growth? In particular, what is the right countercyclical approach to take to best situate the economy for future growth? I shall indicate during US, Amera's economy growth occurs, then economists can attempt to apply customer choice theory to solve US itself country's consumer problems more easier.

In no small part, the question comes down to interpretations of charts like the one at right. On the one hand, long and deep downturns seem to have almost no effect on the long-term rate of growth. On the other hand, in the long run we're all dead, and those who live during an extended period of economic weakness suffer for it. Meanwhile, it's also difficult to see where high debt levels influence the long-run rate of growth, at least where this chart is concerned.

During to the medium-term growth stage, is the bigger threat to American growth rates a market revolt against American debt levels? Or is it structural unemployment stemming from the slow, jobless recovery? Or is the cyclical shortfall in public investment? Or something else entirely?Of course, there's no real reason one has to choose a problem to address at the expense of others. More aggressive monetary expansion could make the finding of a solution to all these problems easier, but the Fed is unwilling to oblige me on this score. It may well be concerned that lack of fiscal discipline will lead to increasing inflation expectations, making its job harder (but then fiscal problems are treaceable to growth). If that is the worry, however, one has to ask why the Congress has been unable to strike a deal for $20 billion in stimulus this year for $80 billion in fiscal tightening in a year or two (fill in whatever amounts you wish). But the outlook for the American economy vis-a-vis any number of potential crises will hinge on growth, and growth will hinge on the ability of private business to exploit promising opportunities as they arise. And the question is: what's likely to hurt that ability most? High interest rates? Lack of consumer demand? A shortage of adequately prepared workers? Right now firms appear to be most worried about demand shortfalls. So how much can you boost demand without making the primary fear high interest rates? A lot, if the expansion is on the monetary side.

● How to spply consumer choice theory to predict Consumer Behavior Marketing at Apple Computer

During US economy growth, Apply computer applies consumer choice theory to solve its computer buyers' choice problems among different kinds of brand computer competitors. Have you ever wondered why Apple is so successful? They were not the first company to invent the personal computer, portable music device, the tablet, the smartphone, software to download music, or the set-top box to name a few. Apple has amassed a brand loyal following like no other brand backed by significant sales, market share, and profitability. So, how does Apple do it? What's the secret behind their success?

Marketing using consumer behavior insight is how Apple succeeds. Even though Steve Jobs and Apple, did not use consumer research in the initial development of most products, consumer behavior plays a huge role in their marketing and ultimately the success of the company. Once a consumer purchases a product or downloads iTunes Apple has access to data the company leverages. Apple uses this information to gain significant insight into the consumer and what drives purchase behavior.

Consumer behavior marketing is an essential ingredient in the current business climate. The companies that apply this type of marketing well have a distinct competitive advantage that distances them from their rivals. Consumer behavior research is the primary driver at the core of any good strategy. Research provides actionable insight and ensures business success.

If you answer no to the following questions, this post is for you?

Are you applying consumer behavior marketing currently?

Have you conducted consumer behavior research within the last two years?

Do you have consumer behavior marketing in your marketing plan with well-defined marketing strategies and tactics?

Are you achieving the maximum results for your organization?

Every business has a target audience and consumer behavior marketing provides the fundamental methods for understanding your target. Consumer behavior research provides the underlying element that drives quality strategies and ensures business results.

"Marketing is understanding your buyers really, really well. Then creating valuable products, services, and information especially for them to help solve their problems."

The organizations that have an intimate understanding of their target audience possess a competitive advantage over those that do not. Establishing a one-to-one relationship and thorough knowledge of your target audience is a core responsibility for business in the 21st century and beyond. Regardless if you are B2B, B2C, B2G or a hybrid organization you have a target audience. The information in this post can be applied to any business type. This post focuses on Apple (B2C) employing consumer behavior marketing as a critical ingredient for their success.

Hence, Apply computer shops have several computer teachers to teach any visitors how to use its laptops, hen they enquire its any computer salespeople. Due to its salespeople had been trained to learn how to use the different kinds of laptops. So, anyone enquires them, they can answer their enquires concern any computer questions immediately. Then, they will feel Apple laptops are the first choice to compare other kinds of laptops brands. It is one salespeople answering strategies to persuade any Apple computer visitors to feel its any laptops are the first or preference choice to compare its competitors in this computer market, so customer choice economic theory is the most suitable strategy to solve Apple computer's customer individual purchase decision problem.

● Microeconomics Models and Theories solve customer problems

Microeconomics is concerned with the economic decisions and actions of individuals and firms. Within the broad church of microeconomics, there are different theories that emphasise certain assumptions and expectations of economic behaviour. The most important theory is neo-classical theory, which places emphasis on free-markets and the assumption individuals are rational and seek to maximise utility. However, there are many critiques of the neo-classical model, arguing economics is more complex with issues of market failure and irrational behaviour.

Pre-classical microeconomic theory

Before, Adam Smith, economics was more disparate with no commanding overall theory. Philosophers like Aristotle and Plato made references to issues in economics such as division of labour. The dominant ideas, pre-classical economics, were based on theories of mercantilism – the idea a nation should try to accumulate gold.

Classical microeconomic theory

Classical microeconomic theory was developed by Adam Smith (Wealth of Nations, 1776) and later economists, such as David Ricardo The essential aspect of classical microeconomic theory include:

Adam Smith mentioned the 'invisible hand of the market.' He noted how when people act out of self-interest, markets tend to provide goods and services which are demanded by the population. It needed no central price setting, but market forces responded to changes in demand and supply, e.g. a shortage pushes up the price and causes demand to fall.

Smith also investigated topics such as the division of labour, specialisation and economies of scale. The early classical economists emphasised the importance of costs to firms and consumers.

Utility maximisation

An important development of classical economics towards the end of the nineteenth century is the concept of utility maximisation. The concept of utility was developed by philosophers/economists – Jeremy Bentham and John Stuart Mill. In microeconomic theory, it was believed a consumer will buy goods depending on the marginal utility (satisfaction) they get from the good. This theory assumes consumers are rational and seeking to maximise the satisfaction they get.

Neo-classical theory

Neo-classical theory is a modern re-interpretation of classical economics of the nineteenth century. Neo-classical theory places importance on markets, but developed new ideas, especially regarding utility and rational choice theory. Elements of neo-classical theory.

1. Market distribution of goods and services.

2.R ational choice theory. This is the idea individuals hold rational preferences and make rational choices; seeking to maximise their outcomes – be it profit, wages, consumption or investment.

3. People act independently and make use of available information.

4. Marginalism. In neo-classical economics, more emphasis was placed on concepts of marginal utility and marginal cost. We make choices depending on satisfaction we get from one extra unit of a good.

Economists such as Carl Menger, William Stanley Jevons and Marie-Esprit-L?on Walras. and Alfred Marshall developed ideas such as diminishing marginal utility. Many of these neo-classical economic theories were brought together in Alfred Marshall's very influential textbook, Principles of Economics. (1890)

?Note there is some blurring between classical economics and neo-classical economics.

?Neo-classical economics has also come to mean 'orthodox economic theory. To a large extent, it has incorporated new developments in microeconomics, such as theories of market failure, market structure and econometrics.

Theories of Market failure

Neo-classical economics has become associated with a belief in the efficiency of markets. However, microeconomic theory has also incorporated the criticisms and limitations of free-markets. Monopoly. Adam Smith was well aware of the problem of monopolies and how firms could use their market power to set excessive prices. Imperfect competition. In the 1930s, Joan Robinson developed a model of imperfect competition, an awareness many markets were somewhere between monopoly and perfect competition often assumed in neo-classical economics. Externalities. Developed by Arthur C.Pigou in

The Economics of Welfare (1920) this is the awareness production and consumption decisions can have harmful (or positive) effects on third parties. Therefore, a free market can lead to overconsumption of demerit goods and negative externalities.Game theory. An awareness, decisions are not linear or simple, but the interdependence of agents influences what we decide to do.

Behavioural economics

The most important trend in recent decades in economics is the greater emphasis placed on aspects of behavioural economics, which uses many insights from related fields such as psychology.

Disputes rational choice theory. The essential element of behavioural economics is that it argues individual agents are often not rational and often do not seek to maximise utility.

Behavioural economics examines how agents can be influenced by biases, and make decisions not predicted by neo-classical economic theory. Behavioural economics can explain the irrational exuberance of booms and busts.

Econometrics

In the post-war period, economics became increasingly mathematical with economists attempting to use mathematics to explain models and theories. Econometrics looks at economic data and seeks to extract simple relationships. The basic tool is the linear regression models and can be used to try and predict consumer spending and demand for labour.

Heterodox models of microeconomics

Heterodox models differ substantially from microeconomic foundations of neo-classical economics. Schools of thought include

Marxist economic theory

Karl Marx developed an alternative perspective on economics. He focused on the surplus value created under the capitalist economic system. To Marx, the invisible hand of the market would be better described as the invisible hand of capitalist exploitation of workers. Marx claimed workers did receive their full labour value but were compensated for their necessary labour only – enabling capitalists to profit from the surplus.

Institutional economics. The role of society and institutions in shaping economic behaviour. For example, Thomas Veblen looked at theories of 'conspicuous consumption' and noted how the desire for social status could drive much economic theory. Institutional economics could be seen as a forerunner for later behavioural economics.

Environmental economics Argues traditional economics wrongly places value on increasing output. The most important thing is creating a sustainable environment which maximises living standards. So, manufacturers need to consider how to manufacture their products , but pollution can not be raised as the same time, because human will face to raise cost of living and living experiences to be poor , even food shortage, water pollution , air pollution , death rate raises when technological productivities brings pollution to our natural environment. Hence, environmental economoic theory is the most suitable to solve manufacturers' pollution problem.

Buddhist economics/non-profit goals. Like environmental economics, this questions the assumption higher incomes and higher output are desirable. The theory of hedonistic relativism suggests higher incomes do nothing to increase happiness levels, and traditional economics can encourage society to pursue materialistic goals which actually create more problems of stress, conflict and environmental degradation.

Some of the basic models you might find in A-Level economics :

Price Discrimination

Perfect competition

Price Mechanism

Monopoly

Oligopoly and kinked demand curve

Game Theory Pricing strategies

Market failure

Behavioural economics

ON conclusion, any macro economy theories can be applied to find the most reasonable methods to solve any customer problems in societies by economists as above. So, I believe that any economic and customer and social problems can be solved by economic theories in our society.

.Developed countries low skillful labour

market wage grows up causing

factors

Nowadays, there are many countries still have low wage labours, even developed countries, such as US, UK , these countries have many workers can not earn high or unreasonable wages to be paid the same wage level to any developing countries, such as China, India normal workers wages level, e.g. arehouse, clearner workers. Why do these developed countries still have unfair or unreasonable or low wages level? What are the reasons cause these developed countries employers treat them to pay their wages in these low skillful jobs in the low wage level and the wage growth is slow. I shall indicate the demand and supply theory to explain these low skillful level workers' low wage level causing reasons as well as the division of labour concept and surplus value of labour theory to explain why developed countries, such as US, UK , they still have low skillful labor market wage grows up or increase workers number labor market environment suitation as below:

The first factor is excess labour supply. In economic view, demand and supply theory as well as division of labor theory and surplus value of labour theory may be applied to explain why developed countries' low skillful workers' normal wage level grows up slowly nowadays in long time. Why do many developed countries still have many low skillful workers to earn the unreasonable low wages level to same to the developing countries? For example, Amazon e-commerce profit firm in US, UK warehouses still pays the same low wage level in these countries, these developed countries' low skillful level workers' wages are the same low level to the developing countries' e-commerce profit firms' warehouse low skillful level workers' wages, such as Hong Kong, China. Their UK, US warehouse picking up or delivery warehouse workers' wages are paid about US$28,000 per year in UK, US Amazon warehouses. Their wages are same to the developing countries' e-commerce firms' warehouse wages level in general. Although, they are working in US, UK developed countries, but these low skillful labours wage level can not be higher than the workers' wages in developing countries in general. Whether the reasons are due to that their low skillful level warehouse jobs, such as picking up or delviery job nature factor or other factors to cause their low pay. However, I feel that their warehouse picking up or delivery job nature is not the main factor to cause these developed countries' low skillful level workers' low pay wage and slow growth reason. I believe that the main factor is analyzed by economic view, it means that these developed countries, such as US, UK , they have more excess number of low skillfil level labour supplies, but there are less employers number, they need to employee low skillful level of workers in their low skillful level job market in developed countries.

Hence in labour supply and demand view, due to these developed countries employers do not need to worry about whether they will have shortage of low skillful of labour supply. So, they pay the common low level of wage to same to the developing countries' low skillful level workers. These developed countries employers will stilll have many low skillful level workers apply their jobs to do in themselves countries job market. In economic view, when supply is more than demand, such as this developed countries' low level skillful labour market case, there are many low skillful level workers need to find jobs or apply jobs to do in these developed countries, but there are less employers need to employ low skillful level workers in these developed countries in the same time. So, it must case that their general wage level can not increase rapidly easily in long time.

So, developed countries' low skillful labour market seems same to developing countries' labour market situation. If workers in developed or developing countries are underpaid and exploited, a profit -seeking businessperson would be able to reap immediate profits by hiring the workers away from their current occupatons ans re-employing them elsewhere in any time easily. They won't need to worry about whether they would feel difficult to find any low skillful level workers to work when their age level is low level in general.

Why has wage growth been grown slowly in developed countries, such as US, UK? Although, developed countries have low unemployment rate, many people can find any kinds of jobs to work very easily. But, it is not possible due to there are many employers feel need to create or increase many low skillful job positions. Otherwise, it is due to there are many people need to seek jobs to do. So, the job seekers number is increasing, but the job position supply number is not increasing , even is decreasing in these developed countries. So, there are lot excess labour supply and less job demand in developed countries, such as US, UK. Hence, it explains why their wages can not raise rapidly as well as low unemployment rate in these developed countries, because there are less job positions demand from these developed countries' employers as well as US, UK are low population country. So, their low skillful level job position competition is also low. Then, it causes low unemployment ratio and low wage level as well as slow raising wage growth effect in these developed countries nowadays.

It means that it has stagnant wages in these developed countries. In fact, country -specific answes don't explain why low wage growth is a global phenomenon whose training for the future and career developement were simply not their problem. So, wages slow growth and low level paid to low skillful labour issue is a global labour market phenonmenon in developed and developing counties nowadays. It is very popular to many employers, they can provide in-house training to teach their low skillful knowledge level workers to learn their related-job knowledge to prepare their career development. So, the developed countries' low skillful level workers can learn any tasks knowledge to prepare to do their new jobs when their new employers provide on-job-training . So, they do not need afraid that they do not learn how to do any kinds of low skillful jobs . It will bring another effect, developed countries employers won't have comparison to whom has owned or had not owned any kinds of task knowledge to prepare to do their tasks when they are employed in beginning. Because every low skillful employees or workers will have in-house training or on-job training learn chance to help them to raise the kinds of low-skillful tasks knowledge level. SO, any low skillful workers must have the same in-house or on-job training learn treatmen from their new employers. Then, their wages will not be influenced to be either higher or lower when they enter their new firms to work in beginning. Their wages level must be the same level, none of reasons are whether they are proficient or low skillful level workers. This is another main factor to influence their wages slow growth in developed countries nowadays.

The another factor may be refugee immigration to the developed countries. Because when there are many refugees can apply to emigrate to these developed countries to live, such as US, UK. Then, they will increase the low-skillful labours number to supply to their domestic labour market. Then, it will increase the labour supply of low skillful level to developed countries' domestic workers supply market because these are many low skillful level of refugees workers , they compete to them to find any low level skillful level jobs to do. So, it brings the effect of excess low skillful worker supplying , when these developed countries employers demand to the low skillful workers number does not increase rapidly. So, in economic view, when the supply exceeds to demand, such as these developed countries , low skillful labour market case, refugee immigration brings excess low skillful workers number increases and employers' low skillful level workers demand number does not increase. So, it explains that why these developed countries low skillful level workers' wages can not grow up rapidly.

The another final factor is that technological development can replace manual low-skillful workers. For example, when (AI) artificial intelligence, robotic technological invention may replace low skillful level workers to manufacture or deliver or pick up jobs in warehouses or factories. So, it explains that developed countries employers do not need any manual workers to help them to do above these simple jobs. So, such as Amazon's UK, US warehouses can apply robotics to replace present workers , it can fire them easily. When any developed countries low skillful workers' employers feel that they do not need to worry about the low skillful level workers number will decrease, even they can apply other mtehtos to replace them in any low skillful level job positions.

On conclusion, in economic view, excess low skillful level workers number supply as well as low demand of low skillful level workers number , due to immigration number increases, robotic technological substitute workers' skillful invention, the low skillful level jobs position need reduces, but domestic low skillful levle workers number increases etc. these factors can cause the developed countries' low skillful workers wages grow up slowly nowadays.